Eye of the Storm

Scott Walker is a former Scotland Yard detective and military intelligence operator, as well as one of the world's leading experts in kidnap-for-ransom and crisis negotiation. When hostages are taken, or cybercriminals target organisations or high-net-worth individuals, he's the person called in to resolve the problem.

His debut book, *Order Out of Chaos: A Kidnap Negotiator's Guide to Influence and Persuasion*, was a *Sunday Times* bestseller and has been translated into multiple languages.

A regular commentator on CNN, BBC, Sky News and MSNBC, Scott has also been featured in *The New York Times*, *Forbes*, *Harvard Business Review*, *Business Insider* and *Fast Company*. He now delivers keynote talks and workshops globally, helping business leaders and teams enhance communication, resolve conflicts and perform under pressure.

Connect with Scott at www.winanynegotiation.com, www.linkedin.com/in/scottaw or on Instagram and Facebook at @ScottWalkerNegotiator.

By the same author

Order Out of Chaos

Eye of the Storm

*How to Make Good Decisions
in Bad Situations*

SCOTT WALKER

PIATKUS

PIATKUS

First published in Great Britain in 2025 by PIATKUS

1 3 5 7 9 10 8 6 4 2

A CIP catalogue record for this book
is available from the British Library.

ISBN: 978-0-34944-064-4

Typeset by Hewer Text UK Ltd, Edinburgh
Printed and bound in Great Britain by Clays Ltd, Elcograf S.p.A.

Papers used by Piatkus are from well-managed
forests and other responsible sources.

Piatkus
An imprint of
Little, Brown Book Group
Carmelite House
50 Victoria Embankment
London EC4Y 0DZ

The authorised representative
in the EEA is
Hachette Ireland
8 Castlecourt Centre, Dublin 15,
D15 XTP3, Ireland
(email: info@hbgi.ie)

An Hachette UK Company
www.hachette.co.uk

www.littlebrown.co.uk

To Lisa, once more. The best decision I ever made.

Contents

PART THREE: DOING

PART FOUR: WORKING WITH OTHERS

Author's note

The case studies in this book are all based on actual events. However, in order to protect those involved and to respect confidentiality, certain key details have been changed, including amalgamating cases where appropriate. Dialogue exchanges are not verbatim, nor should they be treated as such.

Introduction

I'm standing outside my house. I slide the key into the lock and ease open the front door, stepping inside. Placing my holdall on the wooden floor, I slip off my shoes so as not to make a sound. I feel the cold under my feet as I take a few steps.

Something isn't right. I can feel it.

It's too quiet.

Then I remember. They aren't due back until tomorrow. My wife and kids are still away on holiday in Spain with her family.

The toll of the last seventy-six adrenaline-fuelled hours begins to hit me. I'm feeling fatigue so deep I could fall asleep standing up. It doesn't matter though. I'm safe now. I'm home.

Ignoring the siren call of the bed, I throw my running kit on and hit the pavement. I need to decompress, and this is how I like to do it. Some people drink, others smoke, do yoga or watch television. I run. Always have. It clears my head and lifts away the fog of confusion, quietening the noise of cognitive clutter that threatens to overwhelm me.

My legs burn as I get into an easy rhythm. It feels good though. One foot in front of the other. Thoughts come and go; none linger.

I let it all go.

My legs continue to pound the pavement as the miles pass by. After an hour or so, I turn back and head home.

I'd spent the last three days helping secure the release of a kidnap victim from vicious Eastern European drug dealers. It hadn't been an easy negotiation. The shaky proof-of-life video, recorded on the hostage's mobile phone and sent via WhatsApp to a family member, had shown him pleading for his life while lit cigarettes were stubbed out all over his bare chest and back. I could see from the grainy images that they'd had plenty of practice on him before pressing record.

While they were experienced gangsters, they were amateurs at the kidnapping game. They had missed the memo that reminded them there's little point in harming hostages. All it does is signal that you can't be trusted and you are, therefore, unlikely to get as much ransom money as you want. And we certainly don't pay for corpses.

All actions have consequences. In a kidnap negotiation, we'll reward consistent, good behaviour by offering more money or making further concessions. Equally, we'll ignore or punish bad behaviour, such as when they make threats or use violence against the hostages. This is why we emphasise that the more they look after the hostage, the more money we would try to raise for them.

The only way I could remain in control of my thoughts, feelings and behaviour during such moments was to observe but not absorb what was happening. I needed to stay calm at the centre of what was becoming a raging storm all around me.

This meant that when powerful emotions such as fear, frustration or anger showed up, I quickly acknowledged and accepted them. By processing my feelings as an observer, rather than allowing them to overwhelm me, I was able to operate with more focus and from a place of stability. Lives counted on it. I couldn't afford not to.

It forced me, over time, to have no room for negativity in whatever crazy situation I ended up facing. Yet life has a funny way of testing your ability to apply this well-meaning philosophy for real. I didn't realise that it would soon be put to the ultimate test, beyond anything I could ever have imagined.

Thankfully, the life of this young hostage had been saved, and he was now being cared for by his family, while the bad guys were getting over the shock of being on the wrong end of a police MP5 submachine gun, preparing for a long time behind bars.

As I step out of the shower after my run, I think of my kids' smiling faces, knowing I would get to hug them in just a few hours. It's all I need in that moment and is the last thing I remember as my head sinks into the soft pillow.

After what feels like a few minutes, a piercing noise rebounds like a pinball machine inside my head.

Stop it. Somebody, please turn it off.

I realise it's my phone making the noise. Shaking the deep sleep away, I swipe the screen to answer, not even bothering to see who it is.

I immediately recognise the quiet voice on the other end. It's my stepdad.

'She's done it.'

'Eh?' I am trying to work out what he is talking about.

'She's only gone and done it, Scott.'

At that moment, I know exactly what he means.

My Mum, on her third attempt, has killed herself.

Unfortunately, events didn't end there. Within six months, I'd also left the police, a career I'd loved for sixteen years, got divorced and moved out of the family home. With hindsight I saw myself as some kind of saviour, driven, subconsciously at least, by a powerful ego with an insecurity to match, travelling the world saving lives and living what I thought was my dream life. Yet I'd been unable to save the one life that mattered most. That identity quickly unravelled as I eventually found myself sitting alone on a bare kitchen floor in an empty apartment the week before Christmas, wondering why all of this was happening.

In that desperate moment, I somehow found clarity. I knew that the cavalry wasn't coming. It would be down to me to step up and find a way out of the darkness that was trying to force its way in. I also realised in that moment that being driven by a need to feel significant would only make matters worse. I had to dig deep and do 'the work'.

Most importantly, I realised I would not let this tragedy and subsequent events be in vain. I would take full responsibility and ownership for where I now found myself and for the rest of my life, no matter how hard and challenging it might be. This included everything that happened in my world, what I thought, felt and did. I chose in that moment to see life as a beautiful gift that demanded I serve it with a purpose of helping and inspiring others to live a life of high achievement as well as deep fulfilment.

Fast forward a decade and my life is unrecognisable, thankfully for the better. After leaving a highly successful and enjoyable policing career, I worked for the United Nations in the Middle East and North Africa, and then went into the corporate sector, advising organisations, high-net-worth families and non-government agencies on how to resolve a whole spectrum of crises, including perils such as kidnap-for-ransom, extortion, cyber-attacks, hijacking, maritime piracy, malicious product contamination and unlawful detention.

I also wrote my first book, *Order Out of Chaos*, which to everyone's pleasant surprise, became a *Sunday Times* bestseller. I am now regularly invited to deliver keynote talks and workshops all over the world, helping leaders and their teams communicate better, resolve workplace conflict, negotiate deals and ultimately thrive under pressure.

If I can go from that dark place where the ground beneath my feet shook so violently, where I needed to embrace the pain and discomfort and take responsibility for what I thought, felt and did, to having a life and career beyond my wildest dreams, you can too. That's what this book is all about.

Many books have been written on decision-making. They often provide a model to follow like a formula – 'If you do A followed by B, consider C and D, then you'll end up with E.' While such books and models can be helpful (I've used plenty of them over the last three decades in the police, the military and the commercial sector), this is not that kind of book. Nor is it a literature review or summary of the best decision-making methods out there.

Eye of the Storm is a practical toolkit to help you navigate adversity, overcome it and make better decisions, regardless of your circumstances. Whether you need to resolve challenges at work or at home, such as dealing with an ego-driven boss, bringing a disgruntled client back from the brink, managing a never-ending stream of demands on your time, having a difficult conversation with a colleague or loved one, or even facing a toddler tantrum in the freezer aisle, this book will show you how. It shows you how to think, feel and act in the best way possible, regardless of how stressful, painful or overwhelming things may seem. These methods have all been tried and tested in the real world and are backed up by extensive research in neuroscience, psychology, evolutionary biology, physiology and practical philosophy.

I combine my expertise with stories from people who have been in life-changing situations to build a collection of principles and actions that will allow you to hone your mindset to its fullest potential and achieve the results you're striving for. *Eye of the Storm* contains simple and effective lessons you can implement immediately, all focused on helping you negotiate whatever life throws at you. These lessons have been learned the hard way. From my own painful and all-too-frequent mistakes and personal life-changing experiences, to witnessing those made by others over many years. These moments were usually when the problems seemed insurmountable, when the stakes couldn't get any higher and lives were literally on the line. If we messed up, ultimately, people could die. Such high stakes tend to focus the mind on what works.

I have had a unique ringside seat to observe how people operate in moments of uncertainty, conflict or significant change. Regardless of what type of crisis I was dealing with or where in the world I was, there were clear themes and patterns in the mindset and behaviour of the people who were able to navigate troubled waters with relative ease and come out the other side all the better for the experience. I've also witnessed people make the same mistakes over and over in situations where things didn't work out, and you can learn from those, too.

You don't need to have resolved a kidnap-for-ransom case or other major crises to benefit from these insights because this book is designed to help you with the everyday challenges that show up for all of us. It doesn't matter what kind of success you're after. You might want to get a pay rise, start a community group or finally have that all-important but difficult conversation you keep putting off.

While you can't usually dictate external events, you can absolutely control how you respond to them. The lessons in this book provide a way to overcome your problems and become stronger and more resilient.

When we are emotionally, psychologically and physically resilient, we are able to make effective decisions consistently and take the best course of action no matter the crisis. While this may sound simple in theory, it is not always easy in practice. It takes adopting a growth mindset and harnessing the power of reframing negative situations into positive experiences. These experiences provide each of us with invaluable lessons for the future that otherwise might never have been learned. The more daunting the challenge, the greater the growth and progress both during and after the struggle.

HOW TO USE THIS BOOK

You can approach this book in several different ways. You might read, apply and master one topic at a time. Some of you, however, will want to move through the book quicker than that – and that's fine. In my experience, when people choose to develop their skills by applying lots of new tools and techniques, they'll go all-out seeking a huge paradigm shift overnight but quickly become disheartened through sheer overwhelm. This is why I emphasise the importance of small, positive actions consistently taken, which have the most significant impact on building resilience, overall well-being and success in the long run. This approach will also make it more likely the improvements stick.

Each section is a building block on which you can step forward to a more extraordinary life. To learn, apply and master these lessons for the rest of your life requires courage and an unwavering commitment to never settling for less than you can be. To demand more from yourself than anyone else.

However, this is not about striving for perfection because such a thing doesn't exist. What it does require is for you to seek out and 'embrace the suck'; in other words, to get comfortable with being uncomfortable. When problems and challenges arise, there is a natural tendency to step back from or even attempt to avoid what is hard or difficult, even though you know it's something you need to deal with. But here's the thing: no one cares. This doesn't mean that no one cares about you *as a person*, of course they do. It's just that everyone has their own dramas to contend with, and they won't necessarily be willing or able to help you resolve yours as well.

This is a good thing because it means you can establish agency and start taking personal responsibility and ownership for dealing with these things. In other words, to decide, commit and take consistent action. It won't be easy. Obtaining anything worthwhile never is. It will be hard. It will likely hurt. You'll inevitably face days when it all becomes too much. All of us, regardless of our background, education or finances, will experience this at some stage. It's time to embrace bad situations and be confident that you'll become a better person for having dealt with and overcome them.

WHAT WILL YOU GET FROM THIS BOOK?

Think of someone who can remain calm in the most stressful of situations. Someone who can make decisive and effective decisions despite working with conflicting or incomplete information. Someone who makes others feel seen, heard and understood, even if they have a completely different or opposing point of view. How much better would life be if that person were you?

What if, no matter what happens, how challenging the circumstances or how difficult the conversation, you were able to operate from a place of equanimity, grounded at the centre of the storm and ultimately bring much needed order out of chaos to the situation. If you truly want to succeed in this way, then this book is the foundation for your success.

How might you go about achieving this? Following these three steps will help you:

STEP ONE: TAKE THE INITIATIVE AND A CALCULATED RISK

This step is like both sides of a coin. How can you use your initiative while sidestepping the threat of things going wrong? The simple answer is you can't. The only way to master anything in life is to be 'forward leaning'. This means, whatever challenge you're facing right now, you need to be metaphorically on the balls of your feet leaning into the challenge rather than being flat-footed or on your heels. If you're not ready to move forward, it's no different than standing still on a moving treadmill. It feels OK for a split second, but then you get flung off the back, face down, looking like an idiot.

Taking both the initiative and a calculated risk is only truly possible once you experience psychological safety. What do I mean by this? Let's say, for example, you take the initiative on a project at work. You weigh up all the risks, but mistakes are made, and the project ultimately fails, costing the business money as well as clients. Ask yourself on a scale of one to ten, how safe and cared for do you feel by your boss and your organisation? Are you likely to be thrown under the bus and possibly fired? Or would you expect to have a difficult conversation with your boss, in which your integrity and good intentions are acknowledged and the two of you focus on identifying what went wrong, how to recover from it and how to make sure the same mistakes aren't made again? In the latter example, you are in a psychologically safe environment.

This isn't some woo-woo nonsense that treats people as though they are fragile creatures, unable to withstand robust

feedback and challenge. It's a fundamental tenet of high performance and you'll find it present in elite military units and the
top sporting teams in the world, as well as in businesses that
have been consistently successful over many years.

All these teams share an unrelenting pursuit of excellence in
an environment that enables and empowers its members to
speak up with ideas, questions, concerns or mistakes without
fear of punishment or humiliation. They operate within a
culture where everyone matters. This allows people to focus on
their jobs without being stuck in vigilance mode. We applied
this exact approach during and after every kidnapping case.
Everyone on the negotiation team had an equal voice and was
encouraged to demonstrate their initiative with fresh ideas and
suggestions for improvement.

It's worth providing a caveat here, as I've witnessed teams
and organisations misinterpret and misapply the term. Feeling
psychologically safe does not mean people are given a free pass
to wallow in the unhealthy aspects of their ego. Nor does it
mean being unwilling to follow legitimate instructions or accept
that someone else may hold a different point of view or belief.

Nor does it mean 'cancelling' them, engaging in passive-
aggressive or narcissistic behaviour to prioritise your own self-
importance or moral superiority by undermining or silencing
opposing views, rather than engaging in open, empathetic and
respectful dialogue. Nor does this 'safety' give you a green light
to engage in well-intentioned but naive and insincere virtue
signalling about whichever perceived injustice or topic happens
to be popular at the time.

STEP TWO: COOPERATION AND COLLABORATION

When communicating with others, one of the most helpful things you can do is to seek some form of cooperation or collaboration. It's possible to get an immediate, short-term result by playing hardball and going it alone, but you can get much further and for longer when you work *with* others. This is not a new concept by any means. Martin Luther King Jr said, 'whatever affects one directly, affects all indirectly'. Almost two thousand years earlier, the Stoic philosopher Marcus Aurelius said, 'meditate often on the interconnectedness and mutual interdependence of all things in the universe'. We placed this approach front and centre in our negotiations with kidnappers and when we communicated with the hostage's family. Keep it in mind if you want to attract and retain clients and customers who come back for more.

You should never underestimate the power of likeability either. Why? Because it's often a two-way street. If the feeling is genuine, it can generate trust and goodwill, lower perceived barriers or objections, and disarm a potentially hostile or belligerent client. This is why likeability can also be a stronger predictor of success in achieving outcomes over the long term, than just competence on its own.

There is a big difference, though, between likeability and striving to be liked. The former occurs naturally when you have good intentions and a genuine desire to understand others. This is something you have complete control over; whereas the latter is when you want someone to like you so you can feel better about yourself.

Approaching life's challenges using your initiative and taking calculated risks encourages collaborative problem-solving. This is achieved through demonstrating commitment and responsibility, which in turn can make others trust you more. This proactive and creative approach can also inspire new ideas in others. It also shifts the relationship dynamic with others from adversarial to cooperative. From this place, you are more likely to explore potential solutions and find common areas of agreement that can ultimately lead to mutually beneficial outcomes.

It's important to note that striving for this level of cooperation or collaboration should not be at the expense of you sacrificing your beliefs, values or sense of purpose in life.

STEP THREE: TRUST-BASED INFLUENCE

Trust is crucial in all forms of communication. It could be said that it is the golden thread that allows you to deal with others in high-stake situations as well as in more benign, everyday ones. It underpins the previous two steps in every way. Like step one, trust also requires facing both sides of the same coin. To be trusted, you must first be trusting of the other person. And here's the rub: you can't wait for them to trust you; you must go first. You can't have one without the other; and yet, how often do we set a higher bar when deciding to place our trust in others than we do when asking others to trust us. To help, you can express clear expectations by demonstrating what trust looks, sounds and feels like.

It is also the number one factor in the success of kidnap-for-ransom negotiations and the resolution of other crises. I know it's counter-intuitive but consider the facts. Kidnap-for-ransom negotiation is probably the world's most unregulated and ungoverned industry, where Murphy's Law is very much alive and well. If it can go wrong, it will. Yet, if this is the case, why is there a 93 per cent chance of successfully getting the hostages out safely through a negotiation? Compare that with mounting a dangerous hostage rescue attempt where the chances of the hostages being killed become astronomically high.

Suppose there isn't a culture of psychological safety in your organisation, team or family environment. Suppose you feel unable to have difficult conversations because you're not able to properly trust the other person. This kind of culture, whether in the office or at home, only increases stress, while also reducing meaningful communication and connection.

Before we dive further into the book, take a moment to consider and answer the following questions.

- **Think of a recent conversation you've had that was challenging, or a difficult decision you had to make. Were any of these three steps in place?**
- **If so, how could you make them even more effective next time?**
- **If not, what got in the way and what might you do differently next time to incorporate them?**

NOTHING HAPPENS BY ACCIDENT

There are several key themes, lessons or insights that are repeated consistently throughout this book. **That is deliberate and I make no apologies for it.** Those who are at the top of their game for any length of time know that repetition is the mother of all skill. I'd ask you, therefore, to approach this book with a beginner's mind. That is, with an open and curious attitude as if you are learning the content for the first time, without letting past experiences or knowledge cloud your view. Why is it important to do this? Because being in a more curious frame of mind leads to better decision-making. And if life teaches us nothing else, it's that knowing something intellectually, such as concepts, frameworks or processes, is one thing. It's something else to embody them at a deeper emotional and physical level, forming part of your DNA and very identity. That's where real mastery occurs.

Be reassured that you're reading this book at just the right time in your life. Everything happens for a reason, and nothing is by accident. You may be at a crossroads, unsure which way to turn, or facing a significant crisis or challenge. You may feel like you're about to drown in overwhelm with no light at the end of the tunnel. You may just need a little help and guidance in making good decisions in bad situations. Why? Because the quality of your life depends on the quality of your decisions, particularly when things get tough.

I hope you enjoy the journey!

PART ONE

THINKING

1

The Inner Game: Harness the Power of Your Mind

'There is nothing good or bad, but thinking makes it so . . .'

Hamlet

What we'll cover:

- **Pain is inevitable, suffering is optional**
- **Beware of the second arrow**
- **Adversity is your friend**

The path to living a happy and meaningful life, regardless of your circumstances, conditions or environment, starts in the mind. It's possible, irrespective of how busy you are or the challenges you face, to train yours. This tried and tested process has existed for thousands of years and is validated by the most up-to-date neuroscience. All the major world religions, as well as secular schools of thought, not to mention the many fields of psychotherapy, recognise the concept that wherever or whatever you focus on becomes your reality.

We can divide life into three main categories: the things you control, the things you influence and the things you can't control. All three are at the core of how you experience your reality. External events like natural disasters, job layoffs, relationship breakups or even the circumstances of your birth may fall outside of your control, but the meaning you attach to such events and what you choose to do in response is entirely in your hands. By consciously shifting your focus and thinking, you influence your emotional state and subsequent actions, thereby shaping your reality.

So, what *are* thoughts? They are subjective interpretations of the world. They can be helpful or unhelpful, spontaneous or constant. Over time, we may develop certain thinking patterns based on our accumulated knowledge, experiences, beliefs and our personality. If those thinking habits become too rigid, though, it can become problematic.

Our thoughts often happen automatically, sometimes without us even realising it, yet they can have a powerful effect on how we feel and act. For example, a friend you haven't seen in a couple of months walks by without saying hello. This situation can be interpreted in different ways. How would you respond?

Consider these two possible interpretations and how each one might shape your emotional and behavioural response:

Version A
Thought: 'Why didn't they say hi to me? They must not like me any more.'
Feeling: Sad, rejected.
Behaviour: You don't contact them.

Version B
Thought: 'They must not have seen me. Wow, I've missed them!'
Feeling: Motivated, excited to reconnect.
Behaviour: You send them a message, to arrange a catch-up.

As this example shows, thoughts are our subjective interpretations of the world. They can be helpful or unhelpful, fleeting or recurring. Over time, we develop thinking patterns influenced by our experiences, beliefs and personality. But when these patterns become too rigid, they can lead to problems.

Here's the important thing to remember, **thoughts are not facts**. They're our best guesses about a situation. While we can't stop thoughts from popping up, we can learn to notice them, challenge them and respond in ways that are healthier and more flexible.

For example, you've started dating someone and really like them, but they haven't messaged or called you back in ages, even though you can see they've read yours. You start to doubt yourself and think it's because they don't like you or are messaging someone else. But you made up that idea without even knowing what's really going on. In other words, you've created your reality – your experience in the moment – without knowing the truth. Left unchecked, if you continue to focus on what's not working, where your expectations are not being met or what you don't have, you could eventually find yourself in a place of learned helplessness, where your victim-mentality mindset becomes your identity.

This is not about labelling anyone as a victim. Quite the opposite. We all have very little control over external events or what happens to us in any given moment. Yet what we choose to focus on and how we interpret it is down to us.

Denying this empowering fact minimises your own ability and resourcefulness. This is why two people from very similar backgrounds can experience the same moment differently. The same person can even experience similar situations differently on different days, depending on what they focus on and feel about it.

Going back to the dating scenario, rather than spiralling into a negative mindset and displaying a neediness that is likely to put the other person off, consider that there may be an innocent explanation for the delay. They might be working, feeling tired or unwell, or just not in the mood to reply right then. In other words, there is nothing to worry about. Remember, over time, your thought patterns become ingrained as beliefs, forming the lens through which you interpret future events.

Your brain is constantly calculating and seeking to balance the energy expenditure required to undertake its infinitesimal functions in keeping you alive. It also uses up approximately 20 per cent of your entire energy budget for your body. Neuroscience shows that the brain is wired to recognise patterns and create meaning based on past experiences, often filtering out information that doesn't align with your beliefs. So, if you believe you're unworthy of love, you'll unconsciously seek out experiences that reinforce that belief, even ignoring the ten compliments you received as you focus only on the one negative remark. This is the power of selective perception, or priming; where your brain prioritises information that supports your existing worldview.

You're already participating in creating your reality – whether you're aware of it or not. Every thought you entertain, every belief you reinforce and every action you take shapes the narrative of your life. The good news is that once you understand this, you can start rewriting that narrative. You can choose empowering thoughts and beliefs that align with the life you want to create rather than feeling stuck.

This isn't about magic or wishful thinking; it's about how your brain naturally works. When you take responsibility for your thoughts, you gain control over how you experience life. By mastering your thoughts, emotions and actions, you can navigate those challenges with resilience and purpose. It may sound simple, but it's certainly not easy. In fact, it can be downright difficult, especially if life has thrown significant hardships your way. But, with practice, it becomes second nature. You owe it to yourself to try because no one else will care as much about your life as you do. As Henry Ford famously said, 'Whether you think you can or think you can't, you are right.'

Cognitive agility is the ability to quickly adapt your thinking, shifting between ideas or perspectives to solve problems effectively. It can be a game changer to help you pivot out of a negative mindset. But, as you've probably experienced, this can be especially hard when negative emotions are running high. Why is this? Picture your emotions as a layer between your thoughts and actions. When you have negative feelings, this layer constricts, narrowing the options that seem available to you. It is the old 'fight, flight or freeze' dynamic. When you're in a state of fear, your options for action seem to quickly scale down to the bare minimum – and they usually don't serve your best interests.

However, when you learn how to regulate your emotions better, that layer between thought and action relaxes, offering more choice and possibility around how you respond to any situation, even the most difficult ones.

CASE STUDY #1

If you can't enjoy what you currently have, simply having more of it won't increase your happiness very much. I remember a coaching client of mine, whom I'll call Jacob. He was a very successful corporate executive who contacted me one day from his car – not any old car, but a brand-new Ferrari he'd just had delivered.

When I first met him, he would have seemed to the outside world the epitome of success. He had it all – except one thing: the ability to master his inner self and truly tame his mind and emotions. He depended on the validation of others to make him feel good about himself.

He was struggling with his relationships and becoming further estranged from those closest to him. He was experiencing the painful reality that high achievement without deep fulfilment is possibly the ultimate failure in life. Like a lot of people who strive so hard for so long, telling themselves that 'when I get the promotion, the deal, the house, the wealth etc, then I'll be happy'. Yet when you get there, the novelty quickly wears off, and you're left thinking, 'Is this it?'

Like most of us, Jacob thought that happiness, pleasure, fulfilment and freedom were end states to be obtained at all costs. When, in fact, their enduring experience can only be achieved as by-products of a life well lived from a place of virtue, meaning and authenticity. He couldn't understand why the success in his professional life wasn't mirrored at home. He was blaming others – it was always someone else's fault, anyone other than himself; usually his wife, kids, clients or the government; taking it personally when things didn't work out the way he wanted. He was outsourcing personal responsibility for what he thought and how he felt.

Over the next few weeks working with Jacob, I helped him to reframe his experiences and develop a new set of more empowering beliefs. As a direct result, he experienced a shift in how he thought about things. He accepted that he was suffering and chose to become more empathetic and patient at home and work, realising that his old superior attitude wasn't conducive to a happy, meaningful life. His relationships with those he cared about, as well as with himself, improved exponentially and continue to do so years later.

PAIN IS INEVITABLE, SUFFERING IS OPTIONAL

In his bestselling book, *Sapiens: A Brief History of Humankind*, Yuval Noah Harari provides a sweeping exploration of the history of our species. It spans the cognitive revolution around 70,000 years ago, which marked the emergence of our ability to think in abstract terms, allowing for the development of complex language and cooperation, and the creation of shared myths like religion, nations and legal systems, through to the agricultural and scientific revolutions, up until the present day.

Despite all this progress in every aspect of our lives, Harari argues that humans are not necessarily happier today than in the past, and that we might even be more stressed and anxious than our ancestors.

So, Jacob was not alone in having limiting beliefs and behaviour patterns. We only need to look at society. What would our ancestors have made of our modern mindset? Fragile, despondent and dissatisfied, despite never having it so good. Consider how, for the last 45,000 generations, our direct ancestors discovered fire, survived harsh ice ages, fought off plagues and revolutions, and withstood the rise and fall of multiple empires of many nations across the globe. They also invented the wheel, split the atom, harnessed the genome and have provided more computer power in our pockets than put a man on the moon. And today? We have trigger warnings and an indulgent self-obsessed culture, fuelled by a heightened sensitivity to what are simply the ups and downs of everyday life: the realities of being human.

For example, go on any social media platform, and you'll easily find those who take offence at a comment made by a stranger on the other side of the world, just because they hold a different point of view to them. You may even have experienced this yourself.

But if we pause and take a step back, we can see that most of the problems we think are significant are, in fact, relatively small. People tend to exaggerate their agitations and get upset at others whom they think are to blame. Their default emotions are usually anger, resentment and entitlement. Yet it is only when they realise the obstacle is within themselves, just like Jacob, that they can become more tolerant, kind, respectful and willing to embrace others.

Thankfully, the pendulum appears to be correcting itself with a resurgence of focus on the importance of free speech, a willingness to engage in dialogue, particularly with those with whom we may not agree, and an essential reigniting of the resilience and stoicism of our ancestors. In other words, you don't need a trigger warning, you need to learn to manage your triggers.

Pain is a fact of life; not everything will go according to plan, but if and how you suffer is down to you. This is why adversity and challenges should not be avoided as they allow you to dig deep within your own Red Centre – that inner core of calm and control that remains steady regardless of the chaos or stress surrounding you. By anchoring yourself to this inner calm, you can manage your emotional responses, think clearly and make better decisions under pressure.

In a kidnapping case, it would be an almost daily occurrence for the bad guys to make harsh threats towards the family or colleagues of the hostages. This might be the sound of automatic weapons being cocked in the background as if in preparation to execute the hostages, or it may be exaggerated claims of their poor health. I learned quickly to reverse the hard-wired tendency in all our minds to act as Teflon for the good stuff and Velcro for the bad. One way of ensuring this happened was to focus on applying zero judgement to either myself or others at any point.

> 'Thinking is difficult. That is why most people judge.'
>
> Carl Jung

I found the following exercise in Dr Emmet Fox's short book (only sixteen pages long!), *The 7-Day Mental Diet*, helped to reinforce this. It requires you to own what you think.

Try it for yourself.

Exercise

For seven consecutive days, think only of positive or empowering thoughts.

That's it.

You may wonder if this is a joke. It's not. Once you begin this exercise, you'll quickly realise how often you choose to linger and wallow in negative and disempowering thoughts, language or beliefs. And once you catch yourself doing so, deliberately or accidentally (and you will), you must start your seven days again from the beginning.

This is such a powerful exercise to help you harness the power of your mind and thrive in adversity. It gradually forces you to break the old pattern of negativity and encourages you to reframe your experiences, developing a more flexible, growth mindset from which you can make better decisions.

We want to increase the duration and frequency of positive thoughts, feelings and behaviours while reducing the negative ones. Which is more dominant will depend on the type and efficacy of action you take.

Remember, no one can put you in a bad mood; only you can do that. If you've ever caught yourself thinking or saying something like the following comments, you're not alone. I know I certainly have.

'The rain ruined my special day.'
'He made me furious.'
'You destroyed my life.'
'It's my boss/parent/neighbour/politician's fault.'
'Things that happened in the past (long before I was even born) still make me angry.'

You can think this way all you like. Something terrible may indeed have happened. No one is denying you that. You can carry on believing that someone or something else is to blame, or you can take full responsibility for what you think and feel. Whether it feels fair or not, it's up to you. This doesn't mean you are to blame, though. Nor does it mean you should agree with or condone whatever terrible thing has occurred. It may have been unfair, unreasonable or even painful. But I'm offering you a different perspective – the choice to take charge of your thoughts and feelings. Instead of reacting impulsively, you can consciously choose a helpful response that breaks old patterns that no longer serve you.

One way to view this is that things always turn out the way they're meant to. One thing causes another thing to happen and so on. For example, your teenage daughter (I mean mine) might be late getting ready (again!), keeping you waiting. You feel frustrated and start shouting at her on the way to the car, about *how she's always late and never thinks about anyone else, and that she is making you mad.* As you're ten minutes late leaving the house, the rush-hour traffic is now even worse, which means you're late dropping her at school, and then afterwards you get stuck behind a lorry that had broken down just a few seconds earlier. Had you left on time, you would've avoided it. You then miss your train to get to an important meeting with a potential client, who was already on the fence about working with you. And now – because you didn't show up to the meeting or call ahead to warn them, because while you thought you had charged your phone overnight, your daughter had decided it would be a good idea to unplug yours so she could charge hers – the client has gone with your main competitor instead.

All actions have consequences, though some are more impactful than others. Whether you like how things turn out is irrelevant. I certainly didn't like losing out on such an important and lucrative deal with that client. The situation you find yourself in is not going to miraculously change because you're unhappy with it

There's a saying: 'Pain is inevitable. Suffering is optional.' What does that mean? Imagine we met for coffee last week and I was rude to you. If you spent the whole week thinking about our conversation, replaying it in your mind, growing angrier each time, by the time you see me again, you'll be fuming. But it's your thoughts making you angry now, not me. Yes, I upset you last week by being rude, but the pain you feel today is because you haven't let it go. You're holding on, and that's where your suffering comes from.

You might say, 'But you were rude first! If you hadn't acted that way, I wouldn't be angry.' And while that's true, we can't control how other people behave. Some people will be rude, unpleasant or unfair. If you accept that reality, rather than dwell on the fairness of it, you can begin to focus on how you can best react.

Why should we not argue about fairness? Because endlessly debating who's right or wrong only keeps the pain alive in your mind, reinforcing negative feelings. How long do you want to replay that moment? Another week? Six months? Ten years? Are you going to stop talking to me over it? If so, it's like carrying that moment and my rudeness with you for ever. We've all seen how unresolved conflicts can last for generations in families – someone said something years ago, and people stopped speaking because of it.

If you can acknowledge, 'Scott was rude', and let it go, your mood and your life will improve. This doesn't mean you weren't hurt, but once you process it, you can move on. When painful thoughts arise, remind yourself, 'It's just a thought', and return to what you were doing. This way, I don't have the power to keep you angry. You take that power back by choosing to let go and leave it in the past.

This is important.

When we dwell on things, we often realise later that they weren't as important as we made them out to be. Whether I was rude, or a client cancelled an important meeting at the last minute that you'd spent ages preparing for, or you forgot to renew your child's passport before a big family trip, resulting in them having to stay behind (yes, I did that!) – do these events really deserve the time you spend thinking about them? Likely not. You have better things to focus on.

This is where you can exercise control: letting go of thoughts that keep rehashing past events. When something hurts you, you'll feel pain, but that pain will pass. When it does, let the story go.

Most of your thoughts are habitual. You didn't necessarily choose to start thinking about them – they just appeared in your mind. But you can choose whether to let them go.

Remember, no emotions are inherently 'good' or 'bad'. They all serve a purpose. This is about tuning in to and accepting your emotions rather than suppressing them. If you resist feeling your pain, it can later turn into bitterness and resentment. Only by accepting reality as it is can you truly process and move through these powerful emotions. Acceptance doesn't mean tolerating bad behaviour – it's about acknowledging what's happening without letting it control you.

For example, anger is a natural human emotion, often triggered by threats to your physical or emotional identity, just as it is to a perceived or actual injustice. You can't avoid it, nor should you. But you also don't want to let it turn into uncontrolled rage or vindictive behaviour. However, when you keep reliving the original pain over and over in your head, then you (not they) suffer. If this goes on long enough, these thoughts in your head will take on a life of their own, impacting how you feel about yourself. Letting go of these lingering thoughts and emotions is the key to ending unnecessary suffering.

No mud, No lotus

The saying 'No mud, no lotus', attributed to Thich Nhat Hanh, embodies the fact that even the hardest of times can yield beautiful lessons and help us find empowering meaning. The lotus flower can only bloom from the dark mud, just as your resilience grows when it feels dark and hopeless, and your suffering seems all-consuming.

You'll suffer less when you learn to acknowledge, embrace and understand your pain. Resilience is the building block of happiness as it allows you to go further and transform pain into deeper compassion and joy for yourself and others.

Pain is inevitable. It doesn't matter how much money you have or what your job title is; all of us will, at some point, grow old, get sick and eventually die. Not only that, but the same fate will also happen to the people you care about. If that wasn't enough, as you go through life, there will also be many challenges that will be painful. That's the reality. It's not all doom and gloom, though. Just because pain is inevitable doesn't mean suffering necessarily follows.

You might be thinking that this doesn't apply to you. You're not the sort of person who suffers or struggles. You might indeed be a high achiever who sees this kind of language as weak and thinks it has no place in the fast-paced, demanding world of your work. You may even think everything you've read so far is just toxic positivity. Nothing could be further from the truth.

Yet how many of us can honestly say that we never become frustrated with ourselves or other people, whether it's your fellow passengers on the bus or train, noisy neighbours or, probably more likely, those within your own family. If none of these resonates with you, what about when you're simply bored or experiencing that little dose of jealousy when your less-qualified, more incompetent colleague gets promoted over you or even when a good friend experiences excellent fortune?

How many of us can truly avoid being taken hostage by our emotions? The ones that make you think, do or say unpleasant things. You may be one of those rare, enlightened beings able to avoid it all. Still, for the rest of us mere mortals, every day is a hard-fought school day. If we allow ourselves to fully embrace these moments, we can gradually learn to step back from the abyss and transform the quality of our everyday lives.

BEWARE OF THE SECOND ARROW

Another way to consider how your thoughts impact the quality of your life is to reflect on the concept of the 'Two Arrows'. Here's the basic idea:

- The first arrow represents unavoidable pain or misfortune, like illness, injury, loss or any difficult event. This first arrow is often beyond your control.
- The second arrow represents your emotional response to that 'pain' and the negative story you tell yourself about it. This in turn causes you to be consumed with additional suffering such as blame, irritation, anger, guilt or self-pity. You shoot yourself with the second arrow. Its wound is self-inflicted and unnecessary.

By being mindful of your reactions, you can prevent the second arrow and reduce your suffering. It's all about awareness, emotional regulation and choosing how you respond.

In a kidnapping case, I would continuously remind myself and others not to compound or dwell on the challenges we would face regularly during the negotiations, whether that was the kidnappers not calling when they said they would or the courier we needed to deliver the ransom money suddenly disappearing.

Knowing that the effects of the first arrow were likely to last for only a short while, you might choose to accept that the initial events were outside of your control and that you stood guard at the door of your mind to prevent the second one from being fired.

In the introduction to this book, I spoke about my mum's suicide, which is an example of why it's important to acknowledge and accept (rather than deny) the pain of the first arrow when it shows up. It's then about understanding that the 'mud' is there to transform your pain into a lotus flower, rather than to dwell and linger in. If you can avoid firing a second arrow, it will develop your courage and resilience, which will enable you to find a way through when life is challenging and it feels like there's no light at the end of the tunnel.

What you think and do affects how you feel

Your thoughts and emotions have a profound effect on one another. So, if you want to change the way you feel, then you will first need to change the way you think and act. Thoughts can trigger emotions, such as worrying about an upcoming job interview, which may cause you to experience fear. That said, your thoughts can also calm your nerves by rationalising that emotion. For example, it's normal to be nervous about an interview but not to the extent of being overwhelmed by it.

In her book *How Emotions are Made*, Dr Feldman Barrett defines emotion as your brain's interpretation of what your bodily sensations are telling it based on what is happening around you. According to this theory, we construct our emotions on the spot based on incoming sensations from both outside, such as the event itself, and inside the body, for example our heart rate or our breathing. These sensations are filtered through our brain, which predicts what they mean, resulting in our own emotional experience and our interpretation of the emotions of others. This happens in an instant, outside of conscious awareness.

Our brains have evolved over our lifetimes and past experiences, making each one unique. Given the same incoming sensations, your own emotional experience and your interpretation of others' emotions may all be different from someone else's. Because the culture you were brought up in is part of your past, your feelings and how you think can be culturally specific, too. For example, the Japanese word '*Age-otori*' is used to describe the feeling you have after a bad haircut!

This theory means you have more control over your thoughts and emotions than you think. You're not at the mercy of your amygdala. Although your incoming sensations are filtered through your experience via your unique brain, you can reinterpret them to mean something more resourceful.

While it's true that your brain creates your emotional experience or interpretation instantly, you can catch yourself and reinterpret the incoming sensations, even after the fact. And every time you do that you change your experience and brain through neuroplasticity. The more you reinterpret your sensations in this new way, the easier and quicker the new response becomes because your brain has been rewired. You don't need blind faith in an emotion determined by your brain, but rather an awareness of your physical sensations in order to interpret them to mean something more empowering.

As we've discussed, emotions, as well as thoughts, are not universal and don't come with predetermined facial expressions or body language, and are only clues as to the emotion and what someone is thinking. We can never know what someone else thinks or feels unless we ask them. Otherwise, it's just a guess based on our experience, not theirs. For example, a nervous smile in some cultures could be interpreted incorrectly as defiance rather than an attempt to save face.

Thoughts and emotions are deeply interconnected and profoundly influence each other. Feldman Barrett challenges the traditional view that emotions are hardwired, automatic reactions and instead argues that the brain constructs emotions through a process of prediction and interpretation (i.e. thinking). Also, both are part of a dynamic system where your brain uses thoughts, predictions and bodily sensations to construct emotional experiences.

She highlights that your thoughts can change your emotions. How? Because emotions are constructed, changing your thoughts can change how you feel. By reframing how you think about a situation, you can influence the emotions your brain constructs. For instance, interpreting nervousness before a speech as excitement can lead to a more positive emotional experience. This is something I wish I'd learned before my experience in the case study on page 26.

In essence, your emotions influence your thoughts, which in turn shapes your emotional responses. For instance, negative thinking can trigger feelings of sadness or anger, while positive thoughts can elicit joy or calmness. This creates a feedback loop, where thoughts and emotions continually influence and reinforce each other.

Feldman Barrett stresses the importance of your body budget for good emotional intelligence. This budget is how your brain manages the energy resources in your body to keep you alive and functioning. Specifically, how your brain is constantly regulating processes such as your heart rate, glucose levels and respiration to maintain balance and meet your body's physical and emotional needs.

The most important thing you can do to keep your body budget in good shape is to ensure you eat a healthy diet, exercise and get adequate sleep.

You can help yourself and those you care about deal with a negative emotion by reducing it down to its component parts: the triggering event and the bodily sensations that follow. You can then help them interpret this combination of sensations in a new way to mean something more resourceful. Over time, this will become easier.

You can also encourage them to describe and label an emotion with different, more specific words. You could use words such as annoyed, disappointed or frustrated rather than just angry. This changes the extent and severity of the emotional experience. To create space and move forward after a negative event: pause, reset and choose.

ADVERSITY IS YOUR FRIEND

Conflict in life is inevitable. Sooner or later, most of us will find ourselves navigating through it, whether at work or at home. Finding yourself in a confrontation can be an emotional experience for many, but it doesn't need to be. Your ability to cope and deal with it depends on managing your thoughts and emotions. Your previous experiences may have involved arguing, rising bitterness and resentment before doing something rash that you later regretted, such as quitting your job or saying something inappropriate.

Resolving conflict, whether at home, in the office or within our community, is a powerful skill we can all learn and apply. We can only be successful in dealing with such challenges if there is trust and rapport. Sometimes this is hard, as we'll encounter so many people in life who know how to push our buttons. You can engage with them by remaining calm, actively listening to what they say and considering why they are saying it.

Facing conflict head-on is crucial for success and benefits your family, team or organisation. Instead of viewing confrontations negatively, consider them opportunities for growth and understanding. When handled wisely, confrontations can foster innovation and drive cultural change as well enabling collaboration and challenging entrenched norms. When managed with respect they can also encourage different perspectives and allow for assumptions to be challenged. This diversity of thought can spark creative problem-solving and lead to innovative ideas.

Recognise that confrontations in and of themselves aren't harmful. They only turn negative if we manage them poorly or avoid them altogether. This is when we allow disempowering and negative thinking to take hold. If we embrace them with courage and an open mind, we can learn and evolve. We create room for opposing views to spark new thinking and turn confrontation into an opportunity for progress.

It takes courage to do this, and in order to develop it you have to rewire your mindset by managing your fear and understanding what your intention is. If your desired outcome is positive and intended to benefit others, it can lighten the weight of any difficulty you might be facing.

How you communicate with those closest to you provides plenty of opportunities to sabotage or strengthen these important relationships. Usually, the former happens when your loved ones don't do what you expect them to. For example, your teenage kids fail to load the dishwasher despite you asking them multiple times.

What happens in these situations is that you may find your-self engaging in 'unconscious storytelling' (aka 'the shit I'm making up right now'!). These are automatic narratives you use to explain away situations, often without a shred of evidence, usually shaped by your biases, fears or previous experiences. You then make assumptions about the other person or situation. For example, if a colleague doesn't reply to your email in the timeframe you want them to, you might start to engage in some unconditional storytelling about how they're ignoring or disre-specting you, even if they are just busy. Making these assump-tions can quickly escalate into an argument, leaving everyone miserable and disconnected.

Instead, use the following feedback process, a simple, four-sentence method adapted from the therapist, Janet Hurley. Using it regularly will help you and your loved ones share grievances in a way that encourages healthy dialogue and posi-tive behaviour change.

Before jumping straight into the four steps, first take a moment to catch your breath, centre yourself and remember that you really do care about the other person, however much you feel you don't in that moment. Once you're calm (or at least calm-ish) do the following:

---

1. 'This is what I saw or heard.'
Describe what happened in one sentence. Share only the facts, like a news report – specific, neutral, observable words or behaviour of the other person.

2. 'This is what I made up about it/The story I tell myself is . . .'
Explaining your personal view acts as a circuit breaker. Not only does it take the heat off the other person, but it also compels you to examine your own emotions. Remember, this is about what *you* told yourself about how *you* interpreted what

happened. It is not your interpretation of what *they* thought, intended, felt or believed. This is you taking responsibility for how you constructed the story in your mind.

3. 'This is how I felt.'

Focus on *your* emotions, then describe them as concisely as possible. Express a feeling and not your theory, belief or judgement. Use 'I' statements.

4. 'This is what would help me feel better.'

Most people avoid this step, but unless you ask for what you want, you can't complain about not getting it. The other person might say yes or no. This is not the moment to enter a negotiation. Come back to it if you need to.

By sharing your story (thoughts – i.e. the meaning or interpretation) and how you felt (emotions), you're shifting from anger, frustration or resentment to an open willingness to resolve and be vulnerable.

It might take a few goes to get the hang of it. Eventually, you'll get to the point where the other person appreciates you for this rather than feeling defensive.

Anyone who has ever achieved something worthwhile has had challenges and setbacks – because anything worth doing is difficult. Overcoming adversity is a necessary step on the road to greatness. Philosopher Edmund Burke said, 'He that wrestles with us strengthens our nerves and sharpens our skill. Our antagonist is our helper.'

Life is the worthy opponent, the antagonist in your story that forces you to grow and become more. When you have the right tools to overcome adversity, you embrace the situation as a helper rather than letting it stop you from achieving your goals and reaching your dreams.

Think about the last time you had to overcome adversity. How did you do it? What would you do differently? Now, think about a time when someone you admire had to overcome adversity. How did they do it? What could you learn from how they handled the situation? Can you apply any of those lessons to your own life?

CASE STUDY #2

The lights are bright, blindingly so. I can't help but squint and turn my head away.

I'm spiralling in a whirlpool of dizziness – not the gentle eddy-type, but a vicious vortex pulling me into the darkness. I grab whatever I can so that I don't fall over.

There's a noise somewhere in front of me, enough to jolt me out of my spiral. I take a deep breath.

I don't want to be here. Anywhere else, but not here, not now.

I hear my name called and turn to my right. A senior police officer, tall, grey-haired and dressed in a matching grey suit, is talking. He's looking straight at me.

I can see his lips moving. Words are coming out, but I can't hear them.

Get a grip of yourself, Scott.

I'm on stage in front of fifty people. It's not the world's biggest audience, but it's still enough to instil fear in me like no other. The auditorium is deep within Scotland Yard, the headquarters of London's Metropolitan Police. Those present are highly trained police officers awaiting a detailed briefing on what they're about to do: hunt down and detain dangerous terrorists looking to destroy the very fabric of our society.

A briefing that I'm about to deliver. My first one.

However, at this point, I'm experiencing a tidal wave of anxiety caused by a fear of public speaking. It's believed that about 76 per cent of the adult population have fears and anxiety about presenting or speaking in public, presenting online or facilitating a meeting.

Tonight, I'm one of them.

To my colleagues, this would come as a shock. My life was going amazingly well. This was not long after 9/11 when Islamic terrorists flew two hijacked planes into the twin towers of the World Trade Center, killing hundreds of people. I was a young, confident, capable Special Branch officer working alongside the British Security Service, MI5. I was involved in gathering and developing intelligence and conducting covert operations to protect the State (and the British people) against threats of subversion, terrorism and other forms of extremist political activity.

To the outside world, I was on top of my game.

The lights dim, but I can still see faces full of serious intent all the way to the back of the briefing room.

There is a knocking sound. It sounds deafening to me, at least. I don't need to look to see where it's coming from. I know it's my left knee banging against the wooden lectern that I'm standing behind. I shuffle back a little to make the sound, but not the shaking, stop.

I reach forward to take a sip of water but decide against it the moment my trembling hand starts to lift the glass, and water spills onto my notes.

I clear my throat, sounding like a wounded or cornered animal squealing for mercy.

For fuck's sake. This is ridiculous.

The next twenty minutes whistle by in a blur. The troops, fully briefed, eventually disperse to the corners of the city, to stop evil in its tracks.

Meanwhile, I walk off stage sweating like I've just taken a shower with my clothes on, my head pounding for good measure.

Mr Grey Suit awkwardly walks up to me and thanks me for the briefing, even though I can tell he's just being polite.

I mumble a thank you and head for the exit as quickly as I can. The cool, late-evening air hits me as I step outside to take stock of what happened. At that moment, I realise that if I want to have a successful career, I need to be comfortable standing in front of others, talking, inspiring, enabling or teaching them, despite feeling anxious and full of self-doubt.

In other words, I needed to be comfortable with being uncomfortable. I needed to seek out adversity and do hard things to develop physical, mental and emotional resilience, the ability to cope with whatever life threw at me, however difficult, challenging or painful it might be. I needed to take ownership and personal responsibility over what I thought, felt and subsequently did, regardless of the situation or behaviour of others. I now do this by regularly speaking on stages worldwide to audiences many times larger than the one on that nerve-racking night in London. I still feel the nervous energy, but I've learned to harness and use it rather than allow it to control and overwhelm me.

SUMMARY

In this chapter we've explored the importance of you taking charge of your thoughts to lead a happier, more fulfilling life. The key idea is that while you can't control everything that happens to you, you can always control how you interpret and respond to what happens. I get that this sounds simple, yet it's not always easy to put into practice. But it's worth the effort because, as we now know, your reality – in other words, how you are experiencing life – is directly shaped by where you place your focus and attention.

To help you with this, we identified 'Three Buckets'; things you can control, things you can influence and things you cannot control. External challenges, like relationship problems or work setbacks, often fall outside your control, but you always have power over the meaning you give them. For instance, if someone doesn't reply to your messages, it's easy to jump to negative conclusions and start doubting yourself (or them). This can create pointless stress and even lead to ingraining a habit of seeing the worst in others, and eventually to a sense of helplessness; feeling that life is somehow always working against you.

When your emotions are running high, remember you have the cognitive agility to decide on the meaning you're going to give them, and can shift your emotional state and thereby what you subsequently do. Why is this important? Remember that negative feelings can narrow your thinking and lead to poor decisions. By learning to regulate your emotions and adopt new viewpoints, you open yourself to better choices and opportunities.

As you now know, thoughts either arise automatically, seeming to show up from nowhere inside your head, or you decide to create them deliberately. One way to free yourself each time you have a negative thought is to replace it with a more positive one. This is not about fighting your mind or pushing away those pesky negative thoughts. It's simply about replacing the automatic (negative) ones with a far more empowering and deliberate one. After all, you get to choose what you think and believe in every single moment, so choose well.

For those of you reading this thinking, 'That's not realistic, Scott. How can you possibly go through life thinking everything is wonderful, when it's clearly not!' That's not what I'm saying. All I'm inviting you to do is to become more conscious of what you say to yourself. You can't control those sneaky automatic thoughts from worming their way in, but you can sure as anything wave to them, let them fall away and replace the void left behind with something better. Over time and with practice, the amount of both automatic and deliberate negative thoughts will reduce, and you'll find yourself no longer being hooked or triggered by people or events as you previously were.

Remember, you are not your thoughts or, as we're about to discover, your feelings or behaviour either. These are all influenced by the sum of your life experiences to date. To be clear, this is not about you ignoring real challenges or condoning troublesome or even abusive behaviour. It is, however, important to distinguish between someone's unpleasant or disruptive behaviour from them as a person. By doing so, you're not absolving them of taking full responsibility for their actions, but they are much more than just what they say or do (as indeed we all are). This approach encourages you to become more compassionate and less anxious or irate, thereby leading to a better quality of life.

KEY TAKEAWAYS

1. You get to choose which of your Three Buckets you focus on. Choose wisely.
2. True resilience comes from mastering your inner world.
3. Embracing conflict is sometimes better than avoiding it.

Practise Positivity

'The pessimist complains about the wind, the idealist expects it to change, and the realist adjusts the sails.'

William Arthur Ward

What we'll cover:

- **The tripwire of judgement**
- **The positivity advantage**
- **Find your lesson**
- **Post-traumatic growth**

One of the key themes throughout this book is the importance of maintaining zero negativity at all costs. This is not about embracing so-called toxic or fake positivity and ignoring the reality of a challenging situation. It's about taking ultimate ownership and responsibility for where you find yourself at any given moment, avoiding judging yourself or others, and choosing the most appropriate language and meaning so that you can take action to improve your situation.

According to Stanford psychologist Dr Jamil Zaki, cynicism is making us sick. In his book, *Hope for Cynics*, he states how, for thousands of years, people have argued about whether humanity is selfish or generous, cruel or kind. But recently, our answers have changed. In 1972, half of Americans agreed that most people can be trusted; by 2018, that figure had fallen to 30 per cent. People of different generations, genders, religions and political parties can't seem to agree on anything except that they all think human virtue is evaporating.

Zaki acknowledges that cynicism is a perfectly understandable response to a world with injustice and inequality. But in many cases, cynicism is misplaced. Dozens of studies find that people fail to realise how kind, generous and open-minded others really are. And cynical thinking only worsens social problems because our beliefs don't just interpret the world; they change it. When we expect people to be awful, we view everything they say and do through that lens, almost coaxing awfulness out of them. When we think systemic issues are prevalent in society, we'll seek out and interpret circumstances to fit this narrative rather than being more objective. While the world may be far from perfect, it's not that bad. We often fail to acknowledge how frequently things actually do go well. But this viewpoint is unlikely to sit well with a lot of people because, if they accept it, who will they blame or abdicate responsibility to for their lot in life?

I know some of you will want to jump in here with, 'Yes, but what about . . .'

By any measure, the world is still a better place for the greatest number of people than at any time in history (go dig out those old textbooks and check for yourself). The fact that the world has slowly but surely got better means that, despite what the doom-mongers and naysayers say, the future is likely to be so too. Zaki argues that cynicism is a disease with a history, symptoms and, thankfully, a cure.

In a similar vein, Hans Rosling in *Factfulness: Ten Reasons We're Wrong About the World – and Why Things are Better Than You Think* says, 'Step-by-step, year-by-year, the world is improving. Not on every single measure every single year, but as a rule. Though the world faces huge challenges, we have made tremendous progress. This is the fact-based worldview.'

One example of this is that people are living much longer. Improved working conditions, reduced smoking rates and improved healthcare have all contributed to increasing life expectancy from generation to generation. In 1800, if you managed to reach the dizzying old age of forty you were one of the lucky ones. By 1950, that had risen to seventy and in 2015 it was eighty. It continues to rise steadily.

So, forget the click-bait doom you see online or in the mainstream press. Society is not plunging into all-out civil war anytime soon, nor is the planet about to spontaneously combust. Notwithstanding the ever-present and real challenges people face every day, when looking back through the lens of history, you'll find that we've never had it so good.

In this chapter we will explore various ways in which you can deal with your problems from a position of virtue and strength. It is well established that a positive mindset cultivates resilience. It enables you to bounce back from setbacks and overcome obstacles more effectively. By adopting a positive mindset, you can also overcome adversity more effectively and create a robust and agile framework for personal improvement and success.

Within a work environment, employees with a positive outlook view challenges as opportunities for growth and learning, leading them to develop better coping mechanisms for handling stress and adversity.

How do you overcome adversity? Through regular practice, of course. Often, it is more about how you frame the things that happen to you than the actual things that occur. By taking a step back and positively reframing the challenge, you can catch your negative self-talk and replace it with a more empowering belief. By doing so, you'll move towards achieving your goals and find it easier to overcome the weariness and negativity along the way.

This is not about denying powerful thoughts or emotions when they show up. It's about turning to face them head-on, stepping in and fully embracing them. By not shying away, you allow them to work their way through and experience them fully. Feel the feeling but drop any story as to why you're feeling it. Allow the thoughts to just come and go. It has nothing to do with anyone you might want to blame for causing the intense emotions, but everything to do with you. Once you've allowed it all to settle, you can reframe your experience and be more Teflon for the negative and Velcro for the positive. This will allow you to think more clearly and make the best decision possible in that moment.

Research also suggests that optimists are healthier, live longer, perform better and have increased motivation and job satisfaction. A Harvard-led study involving a diverse population group found that individuals with higher levels of optimism were more likely to achieve 'exceptional longevity' (living to age eighty-five or older). This was true even after controlling for factors like chronic illness, depression and lifestyle habits. The study also showed how optimists tend to approach and overcome challenges with resilience and are also better at regulating emotions. This helps them to maintain focus and productivity even during setbacks.

The type of optimism we want to strive for is not of the naive kind but of the wise variety, which we'll return to later.

Imagine the difficulty a kidnap negotiator faces walking into the home of someone who has been taken hostage. One of the first things they'll do is sit down with the distraught family and try to get them into a more positive (and realistic) mindset. Why do this? Because it's been scientifically proven that we make better decisions when we're in a positive frame of mind. In life-or-death situations, where a wrong decision can be fatal, you want all the positivity you can get. Not to give people false hope, but a steely determination that if we focus and apply ourselves then we increase our chances of succeeding. This kind of positivity can benefit all areas of our life.

CASE STUDY #1

In a heart-wrenching missing-person case in the Middle East, David, a long-in-the-tooth negotiator, finds himself alongside the distraught family of a journalist, Max, who has gone missing, having spent months reporting on the corrupt government. It is suspected he has been taken by the regime or perhaps by a dangerous group aligned with it. David is not only tasked with securing the safe release of a beloved family member but also navigating the delicate terrain of supporting and liaising with the journalist's parents and sister.

As the situation unfolds, David recognises the importance of maintaining open communication and providing unwavering support to family members grappling with fear and uncertainty. Understanding that empathy, if properly used, is like a Swiss Army knife in communicating effectively, David approaches the family with compassion, positivity and understanding, offering a steady presence amid the turmoil. He listens attentively to their concerns, validates their emotions and provides reassurance that every effort is being made to secure Max's safe return.

For three weeks, David works hard at encouraging the family to adopt an unwavering positive mindset. Why does he need to do this? Is it even appropriate, considering the circumstances?

The most effective way that the family can support Max from afar is by remaining as positive as they can about what is a highly volatile and unpredictable situation. Neuroscience studies using fMRI scans have shown that positive emotions increase activation in the prefrontal cortex part of our brain, which is associated with higher-order cognitive functions like decision-making, planning, risk management and impulse control.

When people are in a positive mood, they tend to have greater cognitive flexibility, which allows them to consider a wider range of solutions and perspectives. As we can all attest, stress in our lives, let alone in a kidnapping, can impair this part of our brain leading to poor, even irrational, decision-making. Whereas being in a positive emotional state reduces stress and improves how the pre-frontal cortex works.

Understanding the family's craving for information and updates, David also maintains transparent communication channels, providing regular updates on the negotiation's progress without revealing anything that might jeopardise it.

In moments of despair and anguish, David remains a pillar of strength for the family, offering comfort and encouragement, and reminding them to hold onto hope even in the darkest times. David not only forges a bond of trust and camaraderie with the hostage's family but also provides them with a lifeline of hope throughout the kidnapping crisis. This, in turn, helps them remain positive.

Ultimately, David's dedication to supporting and uplifting the family is pivotal in successfully resolving the ordeal, demonstrating the profound impact of 'doing' empathy and remaining positive in times of crisis. Not long afterwards, Max is released, stumbling into the noisy and dusty street; blinking in the harsh, blinding light of the midday sun. A few hours later, he is sat with his family, grateful to be with them all again. David, meanwhile, has already said his goodbyes and is on the next flight out of the country, and on to his next case.

THE TRIPWIRE OF JUDGEMENT

Judgement impacts the quality of your decision-making as it often reinforces your biases, making it harder for you to see the person or situation in front of you as clearly and objectively as you should. This is why it's important to be mindful of any feelings of 'againstness' or a sense of righteousness showing up in your beliefs or decisions. It is these rigid, absolute mindsets, no matter how virtuous or worthy they may seem, that ultimately lead you to suffer. This happens because such beliefs are infused with judgement, however much you try to dilute or disguise it.

Let's look at an easy example. As I've got older, I confess I've turned into a bit of a coffee snob. I can be quite particular as to how I like my 'long black' a certain way. I can also find myself tiring of having to explain for the nth time that, 'no, it's not the same as an Americano because . . .' Now, imagine if I allowed my judgement to increase to the extent that I believed this type of coffee is the best and the only one worth having, while hating all the other types because they're just awful and shouldn't be allowed. In fact, people who do like these other types of coffee are stupid people and should be publicly named, shamed and hounded out of their livelihoods because of their 'wrong' beliefs about coffee.

Judging yourself, others or situations often comes from your ego. If left unchecked, this can turn toxic because it's usually fuelled by strong negative emotions mixed with self-righteousness and rigid beliefs about how people should or shouldn't behave.

Think my coffee example is a little far-fetched? Well, in the grand scheme of things, my inability to appreciate other kinds of hot beverages is pretty low on the scale of life's important issues, even if it does make me a bit of a bore. But what if I replaced the topic of coffee with race, religion, politics or some other culture war topic? Suddenly we have a frighteningly realistic picture of intolerance. For example, consider climate protestors who, however well-intentioned they may be, choose to damage property or block others' freedom of movement to draw attention to what they believe is true. The issue here is not that they believe they're doing the right thing to save the planet, it's more a case that they believe their cause is more valid or important than someone else's, justifying their actions through their rigid viewpoint.

To avoid being snagged on the tripwire of judgement, try the following steps:

1. **Observe:** Pause and simply notice what's happening without attaching labels or emotions.
2. **Accept what is:** Acknowledge the situation as it is, without resisting or wishing it were different.
3. **Evaluate options:** Consider the possible ways you can respond, keeping an open mind.
4. **Act appropriately:** Choose the response that aligns with your values and is most constructive for the situation.

This process helps you approach challenges with clarity and equanimity, rather than being driven by knee-jerk, reactive, biased judgements.

THE POSITIVITY ADVANTAGE

What do we mean by the term 'happiness'? Would it surprise you to learn that there is no agreed-upon definition? You can't label it like a table or a car or a plate. If you asked one hundred people to define it or describe what it feels like, you would likely get many different answers. Some of which would actually describe similar emotions such as joy, contentment or ecstasy. Or maybe even bliss, elation or gratitude? The closest you might come to an agreement might be 'feeling good', which is incredibly subjective and not that helpful.

Father Christopher Jamison, a former Benedictine monk, asks in his book, *Finding Happiness*, 'Do you really want to be happy *all* the time? Even if this means compromising your integrity to continue "feeling good"? Why not choose instead to be honest, kind, or courageous? Just these three virtues alone will not always make you happy. They may even cause you to not "feel good" at all, whether through experiencing fear, or even placing you in the path of conflict.'

This is why it's worth distinguishing between pleasure and happiness. Seeking pleasure is a perfectly normal and desirable part of being human. Yet such experiences can only be fully enjoyed if you're genuinely happy and content in the first place. Perhaps a situation many of us can relate to is when we drink too much alcohol. It can feel really good in the moment, but, as anyone who's experienced a monster hangover will attest, it's not a pleasant and certainly not a happy experience overall. Surely, we want ourselves and our children to master the ability to emotionally regulate, to listen and communicate well with others, rather than pursuing a fool's gold of being 'happy' regardless of what it might cost us?

It's fair to say that there's no direct or magical route to happiness. More than likely it's a by-product of several factors, such as a life filled with trust, respect, value and, above all, a sense of fulfilment in whatever you're doing.

Developing your skills to achieve this, while fully embracing powerful emotions and thoughts, and then being able to self-regulate, is preferable to a naive desire to always be 'happy'. Let's face it, are you really going to be happy that you've just been fired from your dream job? Or your spouse has suddenly left you for someone younger and better looking? Or a loved one has just been given a terminal-illness diagnosis? Of course not. Eventually, you might be able to feel grateful for the time you spent with that person or the skills you learned, but this process takes time and can be hard to do.

Picture this: you walk into the office on a Monday morning and instead of dreading the day ahead, you're greeted by positive vibes. It's not just a coincidence – it's the result of a workplace culture that prioritises behaviours that result in feelings of happiness (as much as we can define it). According to SMARI Research, a US-based market research firm, this happiness factor isn't just a nice-to-have; it's a must-have for boosting productivity and driving results. Employees with a positive outlook view challenges as opportunities for growth and learning, leading them to develop better coping mechanisms.

Similar studies by the University of Warwick, Harvard Business Review and Gallup reinforce these findings, underscoring the undeniable correlation between happiness and success. One study found that happiness makes people around 12 per cent more productive.

But how exactly does happiness translate into productivity? It all boils down to the power of mindset and emotions. When employees feel fulfilled in their roles, they're more motivated, engaged and energised to tackle challenges head-on. They approach tasks with a can-do attitude, their creativity flows more freely and they're willing to go the extra mile. In short, happiness fuels productivity like nothing else. But we're more than just machines; we are constantly looking to do and achieve more. This sense of fulfilment in whatever it is you're doing is what really creates the feeling of happiness.

Companies prioritising employee happiness and well-being create a positive ripple effect permeating every aspect of the business. From improved teamwork and collaboration to reduced absenteeism and turnover, the benefits of a happy workforce are undeniable.

How can you harness the power of happiness to unlock productivity secrets in your workplace? It starts with a shift in mindset. Instead of viewing happiness as a nice bonus, consider it a strategic advantage. Invest in initiatives that promote happiness, such as providing opportunities for personal development or simply recognising and celebrating employee achievements.

But true happiness is not just about surface-level perks – it runs deeper. It's about creating a culture based on trust, respect and appreciation, and where employees feel valued and supported. It's not about employees slacking off or choosing what they do and when they do it if that's having a negative impact on the business. It's about fostering meaningful connections and empowering individuals to thrive personally and professionally. And when you prioritise happiness, you'll be amazed at its positive impact on your bottom line.

FIND YOUR LESSON

Positivity is power. Realising that life is happening in your favour, even when it might not feel like it, is key to overcoming adversity and making better decisions. Every event in your life can teach you something. Those who can find the lessons will succeed. Those who blame their circumstances or others will fail. Take responsibility for what has happened to you and how you reacted to the situation. Check what happened and why. Perhaps come up with a plan or establish a process to prevent it from happening in the future. Then move on. Dwelling on your mistakes and failures only takes time away from achieving your goals. As Steve Jobs said, 'It's best to admit mistakes quickly. Then, get on with improving your other innovations.'

Letting go of the past is crucial to changing how you interpret and deal with the present and find your lesson. Your past is only your future if you go back there. Everyone has faced challenges, failures and setback. We have all felt pain and loss to varying degrees. Utilise the positive experiences but let go of the nega-tive. The difference between those who become successful and those who give up is their ability to find lessons in failure. They do so by coming up with a new, more empowering meaning. Then, they use this unique perspective to keep going and not allow the past to define them. They also reflect, acknowledge and celebrate their insights often.

It's unlikely you'll find whatever lesson you need while in the full throes of anguish or pain. Yet if you can allow yourselves a moment to pause and take a breath, you realise that you don't need to fix anything. Nor do you need to get rid of whatever it is you're trying to.

Let's take anxiety as an example. Anxiety is a signal that you are not in harmony with yourself. It is driven by fear about what might happen in the future (out of your control) or some form of guilt or resentment, which is about something that has already happened in the past (also out of your control).

What you can control is taking responsibility for what you

think or how you feel. This is, as Derren Brown says, 'to walk out into the world with strength, not to hide from danger'.

As the things in the past and the things in the future that haven't even happened yet are both outside your control, why try and fix them? Maybe just sit with the feeling. As you do so, become completely aware of how it feels and where it shows up in your body. Let the panic or anxiety come and go – there's no need to judge or blame anyone or anything for causing it, including yourself. Why might you want to do this? Because when you do, your awareness becomes bigger than your panic or anxiety. Your fear is no longer the dominant, most powerful force you experience. Your awareness is. Once you realise you're so much more than your problems, you can ask yourself better questions, such as, 'What patterns from my past are replaying themselves in the present?'

Over time, becoming more aware whenever an unwanted thought or feeling arises in you, and being able to sit with and notice it, will cause the fear to come and visit you less often.

Radio non-stop thinking

Before you can find your lesson, your mind will usually get stuck in one of the world's most popular radio stations: Radio Non-Stop Thinking (RNT). You may even be a regular listener. If you're unsure, let me summarise what they play. It's the station that constantly plays thoughts without rest, almost like a stream of consciousness filled with worries, plans, memories or even random thoughts that seem to play on loop.

Sometimes, RNT's playlist can get stuck in broadcasting patterns of negative thinking without you even realising, as it usually builds gradually over time. These automatic thoughts begin to shape how you view yourself and the world, often in ways that aren't helpful. By recognising these patterns, you can start to change the record.

Below are some common types of negative thoughts that are played on RNT. See if any of these sound familiar. If they do, turn down the volume or find another station to listen to by practising these steps.

Common negative thinking patterns heard on RNT:

1. **All-or-nothing thinking**
   You view situations in black and white. If something isn't perfect, you feel like it's a total failure.
2. **Overgeneralisation**
   You take a single negative event and assume it's part of a never-ending cycle of defeat.
3. **Mental filter**
   You focus on one negative detail and let it cloud your entire view, like a drop of ink that darkens a whole glass of water.
4. **Disqualifying the positive**
   You dismiss positive experiences by telling yourself they 'don't count', reinforcing your negative beliefs.
5. **Jumping to conclusions**
   You make negative assumptions without solid evidence to back them up.
6. **Mind reading**
   You assume someone is reacting negatively towards you, but you never actually confirm it.
7. **Fortune telling**
   You predict things will turn out badly and treat that assumption as a fact.
8. **Magnification (catastrophising) or minimisation**
   You blow things out of all proportion – either making small mistakes seem huge or downplaying your own strengths and achievements.

---

9. **Emotional reasoning**
   You believe that because you feel something, it must be true: 'I feel bad, so everything must be bad.'

10. **Should statements**
    You push yourself with rigid rules like 'I should' leading to feelings of guilt or frustration when you or others don't live up to them.

11. **Labelling and mislabelling**
    Instead of describing a mistake, you label yourself in a negative way: 'I'm such a failure'. You might also label others harshly based on a single action.

12. **Personalisation**
    You blame yourself for things outside your control, taking on responsibility for events that aren't really your fault.

By recognising these thought patterns, you can begin to shift your mindset and open the door to healthier, more balanced ways of thinking and acting.

Power of the reframe

So, where do you go from here? How do you turn down the volume blasting out of Radio Non-Stop Thinking? Rather than seeking to always 'feel good', you may wish to explore the power of the reframe.

Firstly, become aware of the stories you're playing inside your mind about yourself and others. These can vary in frequency and intensity depending on the quality of your life in that moment. Despite how 'real' they may feel, the meaning you've given the situation or person (the trigger) is just made up. In other words, your story probably results in you experiencing unhelpful and unwanted thinking patterns and behaviours, such as how you behave in relationships or when you experience stress. While such stories have no value in and of themselves, it's worth you releasing their hold on you.

Positive reframing involves thinking about a negative or challenging situation in a more positive way. This could involve thinking about a benefit or upside to a negative situation that you had not considered. Alternatively, it can involve identifying a lesson to be learned from a difficult situation. Finding something to be grateful for in a challenging situation is a type of positive reappraisal. For example, after a breakup you could think about the opportunities to meet new people, the things you learned from the relationship and the gratitude you feel for the time you spent together.

Examining the evidence involves questioning the assumptions you are making about how other people are thinking, feeling or likely to behave. You might evaluate how likely it is that a negative outcome occurs or think about how often a negative outcome has happened in the past in a similar situation. You might even think about what the worst possible outcome is (and whether it is likely to happen), and whether you could handle if it did happen. You can also ask yourself: 'What is the evidence and/or probability that this outcome will happen?'

Other strategies for reappraisal include:

- Reminding yourself that your thoughts aren't facts
- Identifying extreme language (for example, 'I will always feel this way'; 'things will never get better') and rephrasing with less extreme words
- Questioning your assumptions or biases that led to your story in the first place. You might also want to try taking on someone else's perspective; for example, if you told someone else about the situation, how might they interpret it?

Sometimes the first way we reappraise a situation won't stick – and that's OK. It's important to try to think about a situation flexibly in different ways until you land on an interpretation that feels right to you.

The following five steps devised by Jeffrey M. Schwartz, a psychiatry professor at the University of California, might help you shift your negative thoughts and feelings to more positive ones.

STEP 1. Re-label: Name the thought or urge as a problem with how the brain works, not something real.

STEP 2. Re-attribute: Understand that this thought or feeling is happening because of the way your brain is wired, not because it's truly important.

STEP 3. Re-focus: Turn your attention to doing something else, like a hobby or task, to take your mind off the thought or feeling.

STEP 4. Re-value: Learn to see the thought or feeling as not important or helpful and try not to let it control your actions.

STEP 5. Re-evaluate: Keep reminding yourself that the thought or feeling is not real and doesn't matter, so you don't need to take it seriously.

These steps can help you manage unwanted thoughts or habits by training your brain to think differently. Remember, your brain puts out the call but it's your mind that decides whether to listen.

POST-TRAUMATIC GROWTH

Your perceptions and interpretations of adversity affect your ability to cope and thrive. For example, two people, Jayne and John, get made redundant from the same firm due to restructuring. Both have worked for over twenty years and have young families to support and mortgages to pay. Jayne doesn't like being uncomfortable. She needs tremendous certainty and control in her life, even though she has no influence over most of it. She often looks for what's wrong and what's not working. After losing her job, she thinks, 'Why is life so unfair?' She struggles to adapt to this sudden change and becomes depressed. She struggles to move on.

Meanwhile, John is feeling disappointed. He accepts that he only has control over what he chooses to focus on, the meaning he gives things and what action he takes. He immediately thinks of all the new opportunities he can explore now that he isn't stuck in the same job. Because he perceives adversity as an opportunity for growth, self-reflection and transformation, John is likely to experience post-traumatic growth. He may also develop new perspectives and priorities and become more resilient. Searching for a greater purpose helps people like John gain a sense of direction and build motivation and resilience. It also helps them make sense of challenges. Finding meaning in adversity can contribute to a greater sense of well-being.

Post-traumatic growth occurs when you reframe your experience of the challenges you've faced. Doing so can make you stronger because of the difficulties you've overcome. How can you develop post-traumatic growth? By working on your skills. Besides the skills related to your profession or goal, focus on other things that will benefit you. For example, learn how to become a better public speaker, improve your networking ability or increase your personal finance knowledge. Honing these skills takes time and effort.

Think of some of the most successful people on earth. They all put in the time to improve their skills and take their talents to the next level, despite significant setbacks. The most outstanding leaders and successful people know there is always room for improvement. Overcoming adversity is about looking honestly at your knowledge and skills. It's about acknowledging your shortcomings and working to improve them every day.

It's also about applying radical honesty to what is showing up for you, such as how you're feeling and the thoughts you're having at this very moment. While you may want things to be different, once you've become aware of what is showing up for you, the next step is to accept the circumstances exactly as they are. Even if it seems unfair, horrific or unbearable. There is no point wishing it were different. Why? Because there is no other moment to be in. You're fully in this moment experiencing it, warts and all. Just as it is.

You can do something about it from this place of complete and total awareness and acceptance. Perhaps you need to reframe the meaning you're giving the situation. You can do this by asking better questions, for example, 'What is the learning here?', 'How can I be more [fill in the blank]?'

However, while this may be simple, it's certainly not easy to do in the heat of the moment. If you haven't already discovered, life gives you plenty of opportunities to cultivate a positive mindset to practise and achieve this every day. You can incorporate the different tools and techniques from this book to eliminate negative thoughts, self-doubt and toxic influences, and replace them with more empowering alternatives.

How to develop inner strength

'You have power over your mind, not outside events. Realise this, and you will find (inner) strength.'

Marcus Aurelius

Walt Disney was fired from his first job. J.K. Rowling was divorced, nearly homeless and struggling to make ends meet as a single mother when she started writing Harry Potter. George Orwell, one of the most impactful writers in the English language, experienced first-hand the horrors of war and poverty. Elon Musk's journey to becoming one of the most successful entrepreneurs in the world is marked by his extraordinary inner strength, resilience, vision and relentless determination. None of these people would have become so extraordinary, or contributed so much of value to society, without the capacity to find inner strength.

Another example is the US Navy fighter pilot James Stockdale who was shot down over North Vietnam, becoming a prisoner of war for eight years, four in solitary confinement. He was tortured fifteen times and put in leg irons for two years. Later, asked which prisoners didn't make it out of Vietnam, Stockdale replied:

Oh, that's easy, the optimists. They were the ones who said, 'We're going to be out by Christmas.' And Christmas would come, and Christmas would go. Then they'd say, 'We're going to be out by Easter.' And Easter would come, and Easter would go. And then Thanksgiving, and then it would be Christmas again. And they died of a broken heart. This is a very important lesson. You must never confuse faith that you will prevail in the end – which you can never afford to lose – with the discipline to confront the most brutal facts of your current reality, whatever they might be.

Developing inner strength has even more significant benefits than helping you achieve your entrepreneurial or artistic dreams. It gives you a sense of peace and meaning and is a well of energy you can draw from to keep you going through the most challenging times. People with inner strength also forgive the failures of others easily, because they know that they can only control their own actions and that their happiness is not dependent on others. They see the power of positive thinking to take control of their emotions and develop their mindset.

CASE STUDY #2

Let's consider an example from a more everyday situation where maintaining zero negativity played a crucial role in reaching a collaborative outcome. During a corporate restructuring, employees at a leading manufacturing company faced uncertainty about their future roles and job security. Rumours swirled about potential layoffs and department closures, creating a tense atmosphere. Those who navigated the crisis most effectively were able to maintain a positive mindset throughout. Hayley exemplified the importance of maintaining zero negativity.

As she sat in the main conference room alongside her colleagues receiving the news, Hayley felt a sinking feeling in her stomach and began to worry about how she was going to pay her rent and the long-awaited holiday she had booked. Looking around the room, she could see others appeared to be struggling with what they were being told. A few even shed tears.

Realising that wallowing in self-pity was not going to help, Hayley took a few deep breaths and allowed herself to feel the tension and uncomfortableness. Several minutes later the unpleasant feelings began to subside, and she accepted that *she* needed to take responsibility (not her boss, the company or anyone else) for what she felt, thought and, most importantly of all, what she was going to do next.

Instead of succumbing to fear and anxiety like some of her colleagues, Hayley chose to approach the situation with a positive mindset. She acknowledged the uncertainty but focused on what she could control, rather than dwelling on the negative aspects of the situation.

Hayley actively sought opportunities to contribute to the company's success during the restructuring process. She volunteered for cross-departmental projects, used her initiative to think of solutions to streamline processes and supported her colleagues with empathy and encouragement. By maintaining a positive attitude and actively contributing to the company's goals, Hayley demonstrated resilience and inspired her co-workers to adopt a similar mindset.

Because of her positive outlook, senior management viewed Hayley as an asset and recognised her dedication and proactive approach. While some employees became cynical and struggled with helplessness and pessimism, Hayley's positivity and optimism enabled her to bounce back from setbacks and adapt to changing circumstances with grace and determination.

Ultimately, the company successfully navigated the restructuring process, and Hayley emerged from the crisis stronger and more resilient than ever. Her ability to maintain zero negativity, even in the face of uncertainty and adversity, benefited her personally and contributed to the organisation's overall success. Not only did she keep her job but she was also promoted six months later.

SUMMARY

In this chapter, we've discovered the power of maintaining a positive mindset, even in the face of what might feel like overwhelming challenges. Catching negative self-talk and judgement and replacing it with empowering thoughts is a practical way to overcome adversity.

This is not naivety, nor is it about ignoring real challenges, but rather it's about taking ownership and responsibility for how you frame and respond to difficult situations. You get to choose the language and meaning that will empower you to act and make effective decisions, instead of getting stuck in a cycle of negativity or cynicism.

By any measurement, as a species we've never had it so good when you compare life today with any point in history. Yet despite this, we still see how both negativity and cynicism are on the rise and are making us sick as a society, with people increasingly mistrusting others. This mindset of learned helplessness is misplaced and unhelpful. Not only does it encourage a victim mentality, but such a negative view of humanity leads us to expect the worse in people, which amplifies societal problems. This cynicism also misjudges inherent human kindness and generosity, and can create a negative feedback loop, reinforcing bad behaviour.

This is why modern workplaces reward staff who are adaptable and who use their initiative. More broadly, society places value on active participation, i.e. people must take part in their own rescue, rather than outsourcing it. We also now know through neuroscience how patterns of learned helplessness can increase stress and depression. The research also shows us how we can unlearn these patterns and replace them by adopting positive habits and a growth mindset. Doing so can improve our overall mental wellness and resilience.

If we want to improve the quality of our life and the lives of the people we care about, we need to first shift our perspective. We must approach the world with openness and curiosity. Having a positive mindset enhances our resilience, enabling us to bounce back from setbacks.

This chapter has also highlighted that in important or high-stakes situations, a positive mindset is crucial for making better decisions. Research also supports the idea that optimists are healthier, live longer and perform better, both in life and at work. Positivity, therefore, isn't just a feel-good bonus; it boosts productivity, too. Employees with a positive mindset work harder, are more creative and feel more engaged. Remember, success is often determined by the ability to move past setbacks, learn from them and keep going.

KEY TAKEAWAYS

1. Whenever you are feeling like you're caught on the tripwire of judgement, observe, accept what is, evaluate your options and act appropriately.
2. Strive to maintain a positive mindset with zero negativity. Replace negative self-talk with a (realistic) empowering alternative.
3. Approach life with an openness and curiosity to extinguish cynicism.
4. People with a robust positive mindset make for better colleagues, friends and citizens.

Wise Optimism

'What upsets people is not things themselves but their judge-ments about these things.'

Epictetus

What we'll cover:

- **Cultivating wise optimism**
- **We're meaning-making machines**
- **Radical acceptance**

One of the few rules I adhere to in a kidnapping case is never to give the family or client false hope or make any promises about what might happen. Sometimes it's tempting to do this, as it would allow me to avoid many uncomfortable conversations. But naive optimism is dangerous. However much we want the world to be full of unicorns and rainbows, it's not. Yet, as we've established, you can still use the Positivity Advantage in your favour. Striving for a permanent state of happiness will not help you live a fulfilling and meaningful life. This doesn't mean you need to catastrophise and fall into a spiral of thinking that no one loves you and the world is about to end.

Life may seem cruel at times, but it is ultimately neutral: things don't happen at random. Events happen as a consequence of previous events. When one of the greatest scientists in history, Albert Einstein, famously said in 1926 that, 'God doesn't play dice with the universe', he was saying that he didn't believe that the universe was random. He didn't mean 'God' in a religious way but was using the word to describe the order he believed to exist in the universe. At the time, scientists working in the field of quantum mechanics had found that tiny particles, like electrons, didn't always act in predictable ways. They seemed to behave randomly. Einstein didn't like this idea that nature was random. He believed there had to be hidden rules or laws that made the universe work in a predictable way, and not by chance. He believed the universe follows clear, fixed rules and thought there must be something deeper that we don't understand yet. While there has been some debate over the years about what Einstein really meant by his comment, what is largely agreed is that he meant the universe isn't ruled by chance.

For as long as we've existed, we've searched for meaning and purpose in ourselves and the world around us. What is the alternative? Perhaps a form of nihilism that turns us into nothing more than automatons, eking out a meagre existence without cause, value or reason; nothing to strive for, with no ultimate goals or higher purpose guiding our existence.

As you work your way through this chapter, consider being more intentional in how you interpret the world around you, perhaps with a far more empowering meaning and greater sense of purpose. This in turn will positively impact the quality of your decisions and the actions you take.

A major theme of this chapter focuses on how it's not external events that create problems for you but your reactions to them, including the stories you tell yourself. In other words, how you think about something determines whether it becomes a problem. And if you think you don't create stories, which in turn influence your decisions and behaviour, you're mistaken. Stories drive your beliefs and understanding of the world around you.

I'm sure you can relate to being constantly exposed to an onslaught of data and stimuli; for example, in a work setting. It would be impossible to function and make sense of it all unless you distorted, deleted or generalised it. The following two case studies show how, when faced with everyday challenges, your brain begins to act in a certain way, which can prevent you from taking these obstacles in your stride. These examples highlight how our thoughts and reactions are driven by various cognitive biases that are common to many of us.

When facing adversity in everyday life, how you generalise, distort or delete information can lead to misunderstandings, unnecessary conflict and increased stress. By increasing your awareness of these cognitive tendencies, you can challenge your assumptions, adopt a more balanced perspective and communicate more effectively with others. This can ultimately foster healthier relationships and enhance your overall well-being.

CASE STUDY #1

A cyber-attack hits a university, causing chaos and confusion among students and staff. The attack cripples the school's computer system, making it impossible for teachers to access lesson plans and for students to complete their assignments online. In response to this crisis, some teachers or students might distort, delete or generalise aspects of what is happening to help them cope with the overwhelming stress and uncertainty of what has happened.

Some students and teachers might **distort** the severity of the cyber-attack by imagining worst-case scenarios. They might fear that personal information has been compromised or that the school will be unable to recover from the attack. These exaggerated thoughts can lead to increased anxiety and fear, making it harder for them to focus on finding solutions to the problem.

To alleviate feelings of anxiety and helplessness, they might also **delete** certain information that doesn't align with their imagined outcome. For example, they might ignore reports of similar cyber-attacks being successfully resolved in other schools or the reassurances from IT professionals that the situation is under control. By ignoring these facts, teachers might feel hopeless, hindering their ability to respond to the crisis effectively.

Some people might **generalise** their vulnerability and fear of the cyber-attack, which could impact other areas of their lives. They might start to believe that the world is dangerous and unpredictable, leading to distrust and paranoia. This generalised fear can impact their ability to form positive relationships and engage in normal activities, further exacerbating a sense of isolation and distress.

In this example, distortions, deletions and generalisations are coping mechanisms for overwhelming stress and uncertainty. However, by recognising and challenging these cognitive tendencies, you can adopt a more balanced and resilient mindset to navigate the crisis more effectively.

Let's consider another everyday example.

CASE STUDY #2

Imagine you and your friend just watched a film together. Your friend thought it was great but you didn't. As you talk about the film, you start to notice something. You realise you're mostly thinking about the parts of the movie that support why you didn't like it, such as the plot holes and bad acting. You're ignoring the good parts your friend enjoyed, like the creative storytelling and visual effects.

As your friend continues to praise the movie, you're looking for reasons to explain why you didn't. You remember bad reviews you saw online and ignore any good ones, seeking out information confirming your initial suspicion, making you believe even more that the movie wasn't good. This is classic confirmation bias in action and a surefire way to increase stress and anxiety if you're not careful.

Even though your friend loved the movie, you feel weird and uncomfortable. You don't want to admit that maybe the movie wasn't as bad as you thought because that would require confronting the difference between your initial opinion and your friend's viewpoint. Sticking to your opinion and saying your friend is just wrong is easier. This cognitive dissonance is real and needs to be overcome if you want to build your emotional resilience.

After talking for a while longer, you start remembering only the bad things about the movie that align with your opinion. You forget about the parts your friend liked, and you might even exaggerate, distort or delete contradictory aspects of the movie that challenge your viewpoint. Later, when you talk about movies with other friends, you might generalise and say all similar movies or those by that director are bad. You forget that different people like different things and think your opinion is true for everyone, further solidifying your viewpoint.

So, how can you avoid these different thinking traps? By mastering a robust concept called 'wise optimism'.

CULTIVATING WISE OPTIMISM

Wise optimism involves maintaining a positive outlook on life while also acknowledging and confronting the realities of suffering and adversity. This type of optimism is an attitude or mindset that can be experienced through regular practice and application.

It is firmly grounded in reality as it sees things as they are, not worse than they are. When you want to feel more optimistic about specific events, you can mentally zoom out to take a broader view. From this new, broader perspective, you can think of a strategy that will not only enhance the experience of that moment you're in but also create a plan for prolonging the state of positivity until after the present moment (or present crisis) has passed.

WISE = realistic, *not* idealistic

OPTIMISM = proactive, *not* passive

Wise optimism also enables you to recognise and accept your current difficulties. At the same time, it gives you the power and agency to do something about it by focusing on what's possible from a grounded sense of reality. It prevents you from looking at life through rose-tinted glasses or, at the other extreme, by doom-mongering and catastrophising.

The lessons in Viktor Frankl's *Man's Search for Meaning* offer profound insights on using wise optimism even in the most challenging circumstances, namely the author's experiences in Nazi concentration camps during the Second World War. Here's how wise optimism applies to Frankl's teachings. He emphasised that even during extreme suffering, individuals can find a positive meaning. By practising wise optimism, you acknowledge the existence of suffering but remain hopeful that meaning can be found within it. By adopting a positive attitude, you can endure suffering with greater resilience and find purpose in your experiences.

Frankl underscored the importance of choosing one's attitude in any given circumstance. In the same vein, wise optimism encourages individuals to maintain a positive outlook despite experiencing adversity. By choosing wise optimism, you can cultivate resilience and navigate challenges more effectively. Frankl also emphasised the significance of focusing on the future rather than dwelling on the past or your present circumstances. Wise optimism also helps you maintain hope for the future and believe in the possibility of positive outcomes, which informs your behaviour in the present moment. By envisioning a brighter future, you can find the strength to persevere through difficult times an empowering future rather than dwelling on the pain of your past or present circumstances. By envisioning a brighter future, you can find the strength to persevere through the most difficult of times.

We know from the neuroplasticity of our brains that wise optimism is a trainable mindset. It simply takes consistent practice and application. It is also from a place of wise optimism that you can positively inspire those around you to take the proactive action required to overcome their own challenges. Focusing on the possibilities, even micro-actions that have zero risk of failure can help. Your team might be facing a tight deadline for a project, and morale is low because they're feeling overwhelmed. You might first acknowledge the challenges they're facing, before empowering them to identify a single task they can complete in the next hour, such as reviewing a small aspect of the project or to making a phone call or sending an update email to the client.

As a leader, you'll also need to take your own action so your team can see you also 'walking the talk'. Doing these zero-risk micro-actions can help build momentum while removing over-whelm. Leading with wise optimism will also result in signifi-cantly higher engagement in the workplace, as employees increasingly look to leaders for (wise) optimism and hope.

CASE STUDY #3

In 2018, Emily had been working at a mid-sized tech company for five years. She loved her job as a project manager and was invested in her team's success. However, due to financial struggles, the company announced a round of layoffs. Employees were anxious and morale was low. Rumours about who would be let go swirled around the office. The atmosphere was not pleasant.

While Emily was nervous about her own position and that of her team, she did her best to maintain a sense of calm. She wasn't naive about the situation, as she understood and accepted that the company needed to take significant action to prevent it from going bust. If that happened, then everyone would lose their livelihoods.

Some of Emily's colleagues weren't so calm. A few panicked and frantically started networking and polishing their CVs without any thought or game plan. In contrast, others deliber-ately ignored the situation, pretending everything would soon return to normal and that the risk was being exaggerated.

Emily, however, embodied what psychologists call 'wise optimism' – a combination of realistic awareness and a hopeful attitude. Instead of falling into despair or denial, Emily took proactive steps to face the situation head-on, balancing hope with realism. She acknowledged the uncertainty and prepared for various outcomes, while maintaining a positive outlook on what she could control.

Acceptance of reality

Her first step was accepting the reality of the situation. She didn't waste energy pretending that the layoffs wouldn't affect her or that the company would magically be OK overnight without substantial cost savings. Instead, she met with her manager, with whom she got on well, to better understand what the company was facing.

Though her manager couldn't tell her everything nor guarantee her job security, the discussion gave Emily a clearer understanding of the factors driving the layoffs and where the company was headed.

Rather than focusing on the worst-case scenario, Emily made a point to understand the likelihood of various outcomes. She also accepted that certain things were beyond her control, but she believed she could navigate the challenges no matter what came her way.

Proactive preparation

After accepting and understanding the situation better, Emily began to prepare. She now updated her CV and quietly started looking online at job openings suited to her experience. Having done this, she reconnected with key people in her professional network who might be able to support her. Unlike her colleagues, she did this from a place of preparation rather than panic. She recognised that being proactive would give her options if she needed to find new work, but she wasn't acting from fear. By doing so, she could move forward confidently, knowing she had a backup plan.

At the same time, Emily stayed focused on her work. Instead of becoming distracted by internal gossip and the company's struggles, she led her team through several successful projects, demonstrating her value. This dual strategy of preparing for the worst while continuing to excel in the moment allowed Emily to maintain her peace of mind.

Balancing optimism and realism

Emily's optimism didn't mean she expected everything to work out perfectly, but she had confidence that she could handle whatever came next. Her mindset allowed her to avoid the defeatism that had crept into some of her colleagues. Many had become disengaged, focusing more on the fear of layoffs than on their current tasks. Emily, by contrast, remained realistic about the possibility of losing her job but optimistic that her skills and attitude would help her land on her feet if needed.

Outcome

In the end, Emily's department was spared during the layoffs. Her wise optimism paid off in ways beyond just job security. Her positive and grounded attitude affected her team, boosting morale and helping them navigate the difficult period with less stress. Additionally, her proactive networking helped her renew existing professional connections and forge new ones that might open doors for her later. Her demonstration of wise optimism was also not lost on her manager, who, when it came to the next round of promotions, supported Emily in successfully applying. This example of wise optimism in action shows how facing challenges with a clear view of reality, balanced with hope and preparation, can lead to a more resilient mindset. Emily's approach allowed her to stay grounded in uncertain times, a powerful skill that can serve all of us, whether at work or at home.

Cultivation of inner strength

Wise optimism involves cultivating inner strength and resilience to navigate life's challenges. It also involves a realistic assessment of your situation and recognising both the challenges and opportunities. Frankl encouraged individuals to confront their circumstances honestly while maintaining hope for a better future. In the face of unimaginable suffering, he observed that those who maintained a sense of purpose and meaning were more resilient and better able to endure whatever life threw at them.

Although you may not control your external circumstances, you always retain the freedom to choose how you respond to them. This inner strength comes from accepting personal responsibility and agency to find the most appropriate meaning in the circumstances. Then developing a belief in the potential for your growth even when faced with significant challenges or decisions to be made. By developing a positive mindset, fostering a sense of inner freedom regardless of external circumstances, and focusing on inner qualities such as courage, resilience and compassion, you can maintain a sense of optimism even in the face of extreme difficulties.

WISE OPTIMISM MATRIX*

NAIVE OPTIMISM	WISE OPTIMISM
- Disregarding challenges - Focusing only on positives - Unrealistic expectations - Burnout and/or disappointment	- Acknowledging challenges and focusing on possibilities - Taking ownership and responsibility - Resilient performance
APATHY	PESSIMISM

- Disconnected from reality and
  resigned to the status quo
- Disengagement
- Numbness
	- Seeing only challenges and
	  expecting the worst
	- Negative spiral
	- Burnout

Cultivating wise (as opposed to naive) optimism allows you to accept that the here and now feels challenging and simultaneously enables you to focus on a solution and what's possible. It helps you emerge from the crisis or situation stronger.

Things won't get better if you simply wish them so. I'm sorry to disappoint you. There is no 'secret' that manifests your desires into reality, despite what you might have been hoodwinked into believing. What it actually takes is to approach each day and each challenge with curiosity, openness and a willingness to explore all the available opportunities, and take focused, determined action. This can only be done once you are aware of and accept your current reality and embrace the agency that you can now do something about it.

* Credit: The Potential Project.

MICRO-PRACTICES TO CULTIVATE WISE OPTIMISM

Daily optimism anchor: Bookend your day
When you first wake up, set an intention. Reflect and commit on how you will make proactive steps towards enhancing your performance, happiness, fulfilment and meaning throughout your day. At the end of each day, reflect on the challenges you've overcome and the things you've learned about the situations you faced, the decisions you made and the actions you've taken.

Team optimism:
Each week, celebrate collective wins and successes. Identify areas for improvement. Check in with members of your team individually. For example, send them a note of thanks or praise them in the moment for something specific.

WE'RE MEANING-MAKING MACHINES

When we face life's challenges, they can often feel overwhelming, particularly when they seem stacked high on top of one another. Most of us fall into two traps when approaching such challenges. The first looks like naivety, wishful thinking or seeing things through rose-tinted glasses.

The opposite of the first trap is falling into cynicism or pessimism. Doing so can lead you to focus only on the negative, and assuming the worst will happen, or believing there's no point in trying because failure or disappointment seems inevitable. Just as the first trap overlooks reality by ignoring challenges, this opposite mindset overlooks possibilities by ignoring hope and potential solutions. Both extremes can disconnect you from balanced, realistic thinking. While naivety denies the difficulties you might face, pessimism denies opportunities for you to grow or improve. So, what should you do? The key is finding a middle ground where you can acknowledge the reality of challenges, while maintaining hope and taking thoughtful action to overcome them.

This is why you must focus on developing your wise optimism amid the noise and pressure when a crisis strikes. If you don't, it is easy to fall into the second trap of a negative spiral of apathy and pessimism. As we also saw in a previous section on post-traumatic growth, finding greater meaning in life and a stronger sense of purpose can aid you in not giving up and overcoming adversity.

In his book *Happy*, Derren Brown describes how we have a 'meaning-shaped hole' because we are story-forming creatures and stories should not meander without a point. We humans are creatures of narrative who make meaning and tell stories about our lives. Brown further describes how if we drift without meaning in our lives, we soon become a pack of symptoms and pathologies. In the most extreme examples, where people exist without any feeling of significance, many choose to end their lives altogether.

Wise thinkers throughout history, such as the Stoic Roman emperor Marcus Aurelius or the German philosopher Friedrich Nietzsche, have advocated that to be happy or to live a fulfilled life you must accept life as it is rather than as you might wish it was. Seek to improve and grow, but only in the areas you control. And despite what you might believe, that is not very much. For example, is it really worth you losing your cool just because someone cuts you up in traffic, or jumps the queue, or that parcel you've been waiting for still hasn't arrived?

Your brain has a model of the world based on your past experiences. It's constantly making hypotheses about what is happening based on your interpretation of what will happen next. These hypotheses guide your thoughts, feelings and behaviour.

William James, the pioneering American psychologist and philosopher, was an early advocate of the idea that our emotions come from how we notice and make sense of the feelings in our body. For example, we don't shake because we are scared; we feel scared because we notice we are shaking. That we create the meaning we give to an experience can be seen in everyday scenarios, such as when a rapid heart rate and agitation might be caused by drinking too much coffee in the morning or standing next to a strange person in a queue.

It's never the environment or events of your life that dictate its quality; it's the meaning you give them. In other words, if you change the meaning you give something, it'll change how you feel about it and the action you then take as a result.

RADICAL ACCEPTANCE

Radical acceptance is about fully acknowledging reality, even when you find it difficult or uncomfortable, without judgement or resistance. It doesn't mean you agree with the situation or feel it's fair, but rather you don't fight against it or waste time wishing things beyond your control were different. Embrace the situation completely, without conditions or partial acceptance. Why is this necessary? Because it prevents you from suffering any more than you already are.

As you discovered earlier, suffering often stems not just from the pain itself, but from your refusal to accept it. It's the firing of the second arrow. When you resist or deny difficult emotions, thoughts or your reality, you create more stress, frustration and emotional turmoil. Radical acceptance doesn't mean agreeing with, approving of, or giving up on the situation; instead, it's about recognising the truth of the moment and stopping the internal battle against it.

By practising radical acceptance, you can reduce the additional layers of suffering caused by your resistance and allow yourself to process emotions in a healthier way. This practice fosters greater emotional resilience, helping people cope with everything from everyday frustrations to profound life challenges, such as grief, trauma or loss.

Imagine you're dealing with a chronic illness. You've followed every treatment and lifestyle recommendation, but your condition persists. It's natural to feel frustrated and think, 'This isn't how things should be' or 'I shouldn't have to deal with this.' While these reactions are understandable, resisting the reality of your illness can lead to even more emotional distress. Radical acceptance would mean acknowledging that, right now, you are living with a chronic illness, even if you don't like it or find it unfair. By accepting this reality, you allow yourself to focus on what you can control, such as managing symptoms, engaging with treatment or otherwise improving your quality of life.

Remember, radical acceptance isn't about giving up or resigning yourself to a bad situation. It's about releasing the emotional turmoil that comes from fighting reality. It involves both a cognitive understanding (acknowledging the situation intellectually) and an emotional component (feeling the emotions without trying to suppress or escape them). Over time, this format can bring a sense of peace and empowerment by allowing you to move forward with more clarity and less emotional baggage. Accepting the situation as it is also helps you move forward with a clearer mind, making it easier to find practical solutions and cope more effectively.

Try this:

Adjust your sails. Acceptance is the ability not to make a bad situation worse. If things are hard right now, acknowledge that. Then, focus on what you can control or influence and put your energy there. Let go of the things outside that sphere as best you can.

Meaning-making and connecting to purpose. Those who make an empowering meaning out of adversity report an increased sense of strength, a greater sense of belonging, improved relationships and an increased appreciation for life.

Reflection. Reflect on what you've learned about yourself this past year. What unexpected 'gifts' have you received? How could you trivialise life's trivia even more?

The Myth of Sisyphus

In 1942, the French philosopher Albert Camus was intrigued by the ancient Greek myth of Sisyphus and published a famous essay of the same name. The myth can help us understand the concept of radical acceptance in our everyday life. In the story, Sisyphus was a mortal who outsmarted the gods. He put Hades, the god of death, in chains so that no human needed to die. When Sisyphus was finally captured, the gods decided that his punishment would be to roll a heavy rock up a hill, only for it to roll back down every time he reached the top. He had to do this for ever. Camus uses this story to show that life can feel hard and that, at times, it can feel like we're doing the same thing over and over with no end in sight.

Instead of feeling hopeless, Camus said Sisyphus can find peace by accepting his situation without fighting against it, however tough it might be This is radical acceptance in action. Sisyphus can't change his punishment, but he can change how he thinks and feels about it.

Here's how this idea can help us:

1. Dealing with problems: We all face problems that feel endless, like hard work or personal struggles. Radical acceptance helps us face these problems without making them worse by resisting them.

2. Choosing how to react: We can't always control what happens, but we can control how we react. By accepting life as it is, we can find freedom in how we think about it, just like Sisyphus.

3. Finding an empowering meaning in hard times: Camus says that the hard work we do can be meaningful if we accept it. Radical acceptance teaches us that life's struggles don't have to be fought or avoided. We can find purpose in trying our best.

In essence, this myth shows us that radical acceptance means letting go of the need to control everything and finding peace, even when life is hard.

CASE STUDY #4

In a real-life kidnap or hostage situation, wise optimism becomes a lifeline for coping with uncertainty and fear. Let's explore how a family might apply this concept.

Tom has been kidnapped while travelling abroad on a business trip. His family, including his wife Jane and their two children, Emma and Michael, are devasted by the news and left in shock and uncertainty. Bringing together the wider family, they grapple with helplessness and despair as they await updates on his situation.

Despite the overwhelming fear and uncertainty, the family chooses wise optimism. They understand the gravity of the situation but refuse to let despair consume them. Instead, they decide on **optimism in adversity** and hold onto hope for Tom's safe return, drawing strength in the knowledge that he is highly resilient. Wise optimism remains a guiding force for them. While maintaining hope, Jane and the rest of the family make a **realistic assessment** and face the harsh reality of Tom's abduction. They stay informed about the situation, working closely with authorities and experts to gather information and assess potential risks. They can make rational decisions and take necessary actions to support his safe recovery by staying grounded.

Despite their anguish, the family believe in **personal responsibility** and take proactive steps to advocate for Tom's safe release. As the head of the family in Tom's absence, Jane takes on the mantle of leadership with unwavering resolve. She supports Emma and Michael emotionally, ensuring their routines remain intact during the upheaval. She continues to liaise through diplomatic channels and seek support from local and international organisations specialising in hostage situations. They regain a sense of agency amid the chaos by channelling their energy into constructive efforts.

The family continue to **cultivate an inner strength and resilience** to navigate the emotional rollercoaster they are experiencing. They lean on each other for support, openly sharing their fears and vulnerabilities, while finding moments of joy and connection despite the uncertainty. Jane nurtures her own well-being, knowing that her resilience is crucial for guiding her family through the storm. Through this self-care, faith and solidarity, they fortify themselves against despair and remain focused on getting Tom released.

Despite the turmoil and agony of uncertainty, Jane strives to **find moments of connection, grace and meaning** during the ordeal. She encourages Emma and Michael to share fond memories of their father, cherishing their family bond. Together, they create a scrapbook filled with letters, photos and mementoes. They find solace in acts of kindness and support from their community, reaffirming their belief in the inherent goodness of people despite the situation they find themselves in. Through their unwavering wise optimism and resilience, the family can navigate the crisis, holding onto hope for a brighter future where Tom is reunited with his loved ones.

By embracing the principles of wise optimism, Jane and her family navigate Tom's abduction with courage, enabling them all to overcome adversity. It pays off when, six weeks later, the negotiations succeed and Tom is released and reunited with his family.

SUMMARY

In this chapter, we explored the concept of wise optimism, a mindset that blends positivity with realism. Unlike naive optimism, which might ignore difficulties, or pessimism, which dismisses hope, wise optimism is about seeing things as they are without amplifying the negative. It allows us to face challenges with both courage and a solution-oriented mindset.

One of the key ideas is learning to zoom out from stressful moments. By taking a broader perspective, we can conceive of ways to improve our current situation and sustain positivity long-term. Wise optimism teaches us to acknowledge suffering without being consumed by it, drawing from Viktor Frankl's powerful lessons in *Man's Search for Meaning*. Frankl survived the horrors of Nazi concentration camps by finding purpose amid suffering. His approach exemplifies how wise optimism helps us see hope even in the darkest times.

Crucially, this mindset is rooted in our brain's neuroplasticity, meaning we can cultivate it through consistent practice. By leading with wise optimism, whether in our personal lives or as leaders at work, we can inspire others to adopt a positive, proactive approach. This, in turn, fosters greater engagement and resilience, as people are more likely to act when they see opportunities for growth, however small.

Frankl also emphasised that we can't always control what happens to us, but we can control our response. Wise optimism aligns with this principle by focusing on the future while acknowledging present difficulties. It's about believing in positive outcomes and using that hope to inform how we act now. The ultimate freedom we all have is the freedom to choose our attitude, our mindset and the meaning to any given set of circumstances.

We also focused on practical strategies, like the 'Daily Optimism Anchor', where you begin and end each day with a moment of reflection on your intentions and actions. For teams, this encourages weekly celebrations of wins and regular check-ins that maintain positivity and accountability as well as areas that might need improvement.

We can become more comfortable with unpredictable, unpleasant circumstances by practising radical acceptance. This is where you fully acknowledge the reality of a situation, even when it's uncomfortable, and, crucially, without judgement. By doing so, you reduce unnecessary suffering caused by resisting what you can't control. It's not about you giving up but about freeing yourself from the emotional baggage of fighting reality.

Through small, meaningful actions and mindset shifts, wise optimism can help you navigate life's challenges with resilience and a sense of purpose. This chapter reminds us that, although you can't always change your circumstances, you can still choose to cultivate a more empowered and hopeful approach to life.

KEY TAKEAWAYS

1. Zoom out when you're caught up in a moment of stress or crisis, to help you gain a broader perspective and formulate a plan to overcome and succeed.
2. Optimism is a choice. You may not control your circumstances, but you can always control how you respond.
3. Embracing radical acceptance allows you to acknowledge situations as they are without judgement or resistance.

PART TWO

FEELING

4

Emotional Regulation

'We suffer more often in imagination than in reality.'

Seneca

What we'll cover:

- **Emotional regulation: What is it? Why is it important? How do you do it?**
- **Harness your Red Centre**
- **Focus on the triggers**

In this chapter you will learn what emotional regulation is and why it's so important to master it if you want to go through life taking challenges in your stride. By the end, you will be able to deal with whatever shows up with relative ease. You'll also discover how your emotions get activated in the first place, which is often referred to as your emotional 'hot buttons' or 'triggers'. Rather than trying to avoid this happening, you'll discover why it's important to focus on the emotions, thereby increasing your distress tolerance and ability to avoid being overwhelmed.

Emotions are a normal part of everyday life. They're simply a physiological response to your thoughts or beliefs. While they're impermanent, they strongly influence your thoughts and subsequent actions. They communicate to you information about external events. For example, you may feel frustrated when stuck in traffic, sad when you miss those you care about or angry when someone you trust lets you down or does something to hurt you.

Being able to identify, regulate and then effectively use a range of emotions will help you deal with whatever life throws at you from a place of calm equanimity. It also gives you agency and a lens through which you can interpret and experience life more authentically.

For example, Christine is facing a significant challenge at work. She's been with her company for seven years, she's good at her job and is well thought of by clients and colleagues alike. She recently applied for a promotion but was unsuccessful, despite meeting the criteria and being recommended by her line manager. The person promoted instead of her had less experience and was considered by many as not being as capable as Christine.

Understandably, she isn't happy. In fact, she's downright pissed off. Perhaps you've experienced a similar situation. A perceived grievance can be hard to accept. You might have felt a constrictive tension in your body, wanting to name, blame and shame the person who was successful, or whoever made the final hiring decision, the company or even the unfairness of life itself!

However, instead of allowing her racing thoughts and emotions to overwhelm her, Christine chose to focus on what she could control in that moment. She first grounded herself by bringing awareness to the soles of her feet, which allowed her to become more present. She then focused on her breath, noticing how the air felt as it came in through her nose, expanding her abdomen, before leaving through her thinly pursed lips, as if she was blowing through a straw. This slow exhalation allowed Christine's lungs to empty completely, thereby improving the exchange of oxygen and carbon dioxide, helping her to experience a calmer, more regulated state.

As she sat there, more disempowering thoughts showed up. Instead of pushing them away or clinging to them, she noticed each one as if she were sitting at the side of the road watching cars drive past. Christine also began to feel a tightness in her shoulders and upper back, accompanied with a feeling of frustration, which she knew from experience was a sign of stress.

Avoiding the temptation to spiral into catastrophising or blaming others, Christine acknowledged and accepted how she was feeling, returning her focus to her breath whenever she felt her mind wandering. As she sat there, she realised that she didn't have to control or fix everything in that moment. It took a while, but gradually, the tension dissipated, and she experienced more clarity about the situation and her reaction.

By creating space, she was able to observe her inner world calmly and with acceptance, freeing herself from being swept away by judgement or reactivity. She realised that while she couldn't control external circumstances, she could control how she responded to them. She recognised that setbacks are a natural part of life and that we all have the resilience and inner strength to overcome them. We just need to rediscover this and develop it every day. This is what this book is all about.

With a calm and centred mind, you are better equipped to assess the situation objectively and consider your options. For Christine, these might involve exploring alternative career paths, seeking new opportunities for growth and development or simply accepting the situation with grace. From this place, you can flourish and avoid choosing the negative and even destructive option. You can work *with* your emotions rather than being overwhelmed *by* them. Even though difficult emotions will arise in tough times, you can move forward confidently, knowing you have the right tools to think clearly and act positively.

While it's true that whatever you're feeling right now is the sum of all your previous experiences,* what is not true (despite what you may have been led to believe) is that we all share similar emotions. You might even believe you can accurately recognise emotions in another person, particularly in times of stress or uncertainty. But can you? Researchers from the University of North Carolina and the Yonsei University in Seoul reported that rather than the world's entire population all sharing and experiencing similar emotions, you construct them according to your unique life experiences, the environment and culture in which you live, and your 'model' or view of the world.

Despite their best efforts, scientists have yet to find a consistent, universal fingerprint for a single emotion in your brain or body. For example, not everyone who feels scared has a racing heartbeat, sweaty palms and an amygdala desperately looking to avert a perceived threat.

Your emotions are unique. Just like you. You experience them differently based on learned responses you have developed over many years. This experience creates your blueprint for interpreting the world around you. Your brain actively constructs your perceptions and interpretations from these experiences. For example, you might hear a loud bang outside your window. Depending on your blueprint, you might interpret this as nothing to worry about because it's probably just a car backfiring. Or you might feel the need to dive for cover as

---

* Emphasised by ancient thinkers from the schools of Stoicism, Buddhism and Socratic philosophy through to Jung, Sartre and others in more recent times.

you think it could be a gunshot. This is also why two people can experience the same situation or set of circumstances, yet both will have a different reality and experience different emotions.

CASE STUDY #1

On 14 May 2013, the Danish photographer Daniel Rye flew from Copenhagen to the Turkish city of Gaziantep before crossing the border into Syria. Over the next three days, he photographed Syrians who were attempting to make the most of their life amid a two-year-long civil war.

Before travelling to Syria, Daniel spoke with a highly experienced and capable security consultant called Arthur (whom I also worked with a few years later). Arthur advised him against going. But, he said, if Daniel did insist on travelling, then he needed to follow certain advice if he ever were to be kidnapped: never tell a lie, create a routine and play the game.

Despite the warnings, Daniel's passion for photography and adventure would, just four days later, lead him down a perilous path into the clutches of one of the most notorious terrorist organisations: ISIS.

On his final day in Azaz, northern Syria, Rye and his local fixer rose early to take photographs in the town centre. They were soon approached and told they couldn't film without permission from the local authorities. Knowing where to go, the local fixer took Rye to an old building, sat behind a black metal gate, that had housed the Assad regime's local council offices. It wasn't long before Rye and his fixer were surrounded by masked men with automatic weapons. Things deteriorated quickly from there as Rye was handcuffed, blindfolded and taken away.

Over the coming weeks and months, he endured poor sanitary conditions, regular beatings, cramped spaces and a lack of food and water. There were also repeated threats to behead him, interspersed with the ritual humiliation of being forced to bark like a dog. The pressure got so much that Rye attempted to take his own life.

After a month, his family received a ransom demand of $700,000. The challenge they now faced was that the Danish government prohibited the payment of any money to a terrorist group.

As described in the bestselling account of Daniel's ordeal, *The ISIS Hostage* by Puk Damsgård, Daniel and the other prisoners did their best to keep their spirits up by playing games and telling each other stories. As a keen gymnast, Daniel also did his best to try and exercise whenever he got the chance.

He celebrated his twenty-fifth birthday while in captivity, receiving a kick from his captors for each year of his life by way of an unwanted present.

Amid the chaos and terror of the next thirteen months, his story of resilience and survival underscores the crucial role of emotional regulation in the face of unimaginable adversity. As fear threatened to consume him, Daniel's ability to regulate his emotions became a beacon of sanity in a sea of madness. When despair threatened to overwhelm him, he summoned every ounce of inner strength to keep his emotions in check. He understood that maintaining a sense of calm wasn't a luxury but a matter of survival.

For Daniel, emotional regulation wasn't just about suppressing fear but also about finding moments of joy and connection, forging unlikely bonds with his fellow hostages. It was about drawing strength from their shared experiences and building camaraderie that ultimately enabled him to overcome adversity.

When Rye was finally reunited with his family in June 2014, after a €2,000,000 ransom was paid, he realised, tears streaming down his face, that emotional regulation wasn't about numbing oneself to pain; it was about acknowledging and embracing the full spectrum of human emotions even in the direst of circumstances.

EMOTIONAL REGULATION: WHAT IT IS, WHY IS IT IMPORTANT AND HOW CAN YOU DO IT?

Regulating your emotions is how you stay cool, calm and collected, think clearly and make the right decisions, particularly under pressure. It is the number one skill of the world's best communicators and a meta-skill of life. Anyone who has mastered their field and become the best at what they do, whether in sports, media, business or public service, can, more often than not, regulate their emotions. The good news is, like any skill, this can be learned and practised.

There are two broad categories of emotional regulation. The first is **reframing**, which involves changing your thoughts in order to change your responses. Doing so can reduce negative feelings and biological responses to your emotional triggers and hot buttons.

In the earlier example of Christine not getting promoted, she might change the meaning of being unsuccessful from resentment or frustration to, 'It's just one promotion. I still have a job and can seek helpful feedback on why I didn't get the role, or it's given me a nudge to leave and follow my dreams doing something else.'

The second is **suppression**, which is counterproductive and linked to more negative outcomes. This is why the cliché 'what you resist persists' is so valid. Research also indicates that ignoring your emotions is associated with dissatisfaction and poor well-being.

Later in this chapter, you'll discover how, by applying proven, evidence-based skills and techniques to rethink and reframe, you can better regulate painful emotions and manage stressful situations and other challenges in life.

It is easy to dismiss your emotions as a passing fad, an inconvenience or even something to ignore. Yet they dictate not only your thoughts but also your whole decision-making process. It is also important when it comes to parenting. Rather than obsessing on making your kids happy all the time, you're better off teaching them how to regulate their emotions. By helping them not to be afraid of or avoid powerful emotions, but to name or label them, they develop skills, which in turn enable them to be happier, to manage life better, and to enjoy greater well-being as they grow and experience the world for themselves.

Research shows that if you can accurately name and label yours or another person's emotions, it is directly proportional to your happiness levels. However, labelling emotions has always been more complex than it seems because they are not always what you think they are. For example, if you said you felt annoyed, does that mean you're frustrated, irritated, angry, sad, resentful or ashamed? Likewise, as we discussed earlier, the definition of happiness may seem obvious to many, but when you use it to describe a feeling, do you mean joy, contentment, love, peace, ease or perhaps something else entirely?

Another example is the term 'anxiety'. Believe it or not, it is not a universally recognised term or emotion. For example, it does not exist in Eskimo and Yoruba cultures, nor is there an equivalent translation for it in Chinese. Likewise, the term or emotion 'depression' is absent among many non-Western cultures.

Previously, a widely accepted theory of basic emotions and their expressions was developed by Paul Ekman, who suggested we have six basic emotions: sadness, happiness, fear, anger, surprise and disgust. Yet, as we've now discovered, how you define your experiences rarely fits neatly into these limited categories.

Dr Feldman Barrett, one of the world's leading scientists on emotions, describes the importance of developing your 'emotional granularity'. In other words, the more you can express your emotions using a more comprehensive and nuanced vocabulary, the easier it is to manage and regulate them. This, in turn, enables you to think more clearly, make better decisions and take the right course of action. You are what you feel, if you can describe it accurately!

You can find a vocabulary grid in Appendix A, which provides an extensive list of words to describe your feelings rather more accurately than relying on one of the habitual six as described above.

You're often told that you should strive to be happy, that it is the ultimate pursuit of life. Nothing could be further from the truth. Happiness is not a helpful goal, yet some governments world-wide have even established 'Happiness Czars', whose job is to raise the happiness levels of their populations and hopefully improve the country's standing in some arbitrary league table of happiness.

It can be argued that such a misconception correlates with the wide range of mental-health challenges that people face today. As adults, you reinforce this falsehood and instil it in your children, thereby setting them up for a life of suffering. It sounds harsh, I know. Because it's impossible to always be happy. For example, imagine a loved one dies in sudden and horrific circumstances, or you're suffering from an illness. In these moments, it would be naive to think that life is full of unicorns and rainbows, and that you should bask in deep joy. While you might be able to overcome such horrific challenges with grace and fortitude over time, you're unlikely to be 'happy' any time soon – and that's OK. Rather than seeing happiness as a goal in and of itself, it should be seen as a by-product of effective emotional self-regulation.

Powerful emotions are part of your daily life. Pretending they don't exist won't make them disappear, and it is not helpful to continue reinforcing a negative and disempowering story on a loop inside your head. Your ability to self-regulate is crucial to how you communicate with others and therefore the quality of relationships in all areas of your life.

For example, if you're fired from your job, stuck in a ten-mile traffic jam or hear that someone you care about has been diagnosed with a terminal illness, you are likely to feel angry, frustrated or upset. You're unlikely to be in a blissfully happy state.

These types of situations are commonplace and a regular part of life. In these and similar circumstances, rather than chanting, 'I'm happy, I'm happy, I'm happy', you can learn how to develop an awareness of what you're feeling and acknowledge it, before accepting this is where you find yourself, however much you'd rather be in a different situation. Sitting with and tuning into the waves of emotional discomfort in your body, while avoiding the need to get rid of such feelings, will train your nervous system to regulate these powerful feelings. Otherwise, you will develop an inability to cope with anything distressing.

While it's natural to feel a wide range of emotions regularly, some people experience them far more acutely, with higher highs and lower lows. This is particularly common with emotions such as anger, envy, joy and bliss. As adults, you are expected to manage your emotions in socially acceptable ways, because when your emotions get the better of you, they can cause problems. For example, you might yell at your kids or colleagues for some insignificant reason. Eventually, if left untamed, they begin to impact your life negatively. They cause you to do and say things you regret and damage your relationships or reputation.

Many factors can impede emotional regulation, including your beliefs about negative emotions. Sometimes, stressful situations can evoke potent emotions within you. One way such volatility can hurt is by impacting your relationships with others. When you can't moderate your anger, you are more likely to say things that hurt those around you and cause them to pull away. Most of us probably regret things we've said or have had to spend time repairing relationships we care about as a result.

There can be several reasons why you might lose control of your emotions. You may be genetically predisposed to these rapid changes, of course, or have yet to see good emotional regulation modelled by others, or lack the skills to be able to do it yourself. You may still lose control when you experience triggers from situations that happened many years ago.

Physical changes in your body, such as exhaustion or a drop in blood sugar, can also cause you to lose control of your emotions. Hangry, anyone? This is why I would regularly encourage the families and colleagues of hostages to look after themselves (rest, sleep, exercise, eat, etc.) during stressful and often lengthy negotiations with kidnappers so that they could give themselves the best possible chance of success.

How you can emotionally self-regulate

You can achieve emotional regulation in several ways when you are under pressure. It's important to find methods that work for you. Here are some that have been proven to work. Give them a go and make them your own.

Create space to feel

Emotions happen fast. You don't think, 'Now I will be angry'; instead, you suddenly feel furious with a rising tension in your body. A proven skill in regulating difficult emotions, which is a gift you can give yourself, is to **pause**. Take a breath. Slow down the moment between trigger and response. Buy yourself some time, even if just for a few seconds. The gap between these two events is the only thing you can completely control.

Notice what you feel

Be aware of what you're feeling. Tune inwards, get curious and investigate as if you were Sherlock Holmes. What sensations do you **notice** in your body? Is there, for example, a churning feeling in your stomach or a tightness in your neck? Physical symptoms can guide you to what is going on emotionally, perhaps even at a subconscious level.

Improving your ability to pause and notice means you can proactively pre-empt whatever is likely to surface. This, in turn, creates new neural pathways in your brain, making it easier to respond more rationally and objectively in future.

Try the following exercise for the next seven days:

1. Pause for thirty seconds, three times each day.
2. Simply notice whatever you're feeling without judgement or commentary.
3. Observe whether any similar themes or patterns show up.

Name what you feel

After creating space and noticing what you feel, your ability to **name** it can help you control what is happening. In the world of kidnap and hostage negotiation there is a great saying when it comes to dealing with emotions: name it to tame it. As we discovered earlier, by identifying and giving it a name, it reduces the hold it might otherwise have over you. What would you call the emotions you're feeling? What else is it? One strong emotion that often hides beneath others is 'fear'.

Often you can feel more than one emotion at a time, so expand your curiosity to identify all the emotions you might be feeling. Then, dig even deeper. If you feel fear, for example, what might you be afraid of? If you feel anger, what or who are you angry about or towards? Do you feel irritable? What is it that's irritating you? While it's natural to want to explore why you're feeling this way – usually to apportion blame to something or someone (including towards yourself) to justify why you feel the way you do – it's just not worth going down that rabbit hole.

Imagine standing on a riverbank, with the flowing water in front of you representing your emotions. Whenever you get triggered and fall in, do you languish in the swirling tides and eddies, flapping around, increasing your chances of emotionally drowning? Or do you haul yourself out and observe it from the riverbank? Or, ideally, you could even avoid falling in in the first place? Wherever you can, observe but don't absorb. In other words, feel the feeling but drop the story about why you're feeling those emotions. It's just trapped energy looking to be released.

Accept how you feel

Emotions are a normal and natural part of how you respond to situations. Recognise that your emotional reactions are valid rather than beating yourself up for feeling angry or scared. Practise self-compassion and give yourself some grace by **accepting**, rather than trying to force the unpleasant feeling away or even cling to it when things feel good. As the thirteenth-century poet Rumi said, 'Embrace every emotion. Each feeling is a visitor, guiding you towards your personal growth and self-discovery.' Whether the emotions are pleasant or otherwise, you won't be experiencing them for ever, as they'll disappear eventually, only to be replaced by others soon enough.

Practise mindfulness

Mindfulness is one of those things that people can sometimes over-complicate. What it really comes down to is simply expanding your focus and awareness of what is happening both inside and outside of you. Doing so enables you to be present in the moment and home in on what really matters, rather than something that has happened in the past or has not even happened yet (and might never). Practising mindfulness can help you stay calm and avoid engaging in negative thoughts when you are in emotional pain.

If you face your unpleasant feelings with care, compassion and nonviolence, you can transform them into healthy, nourishing energy. Mindful observation can also illuminate your unpleasant feelings, offering insight and understanding into yourself and others. An example of how you might practise mindfulness in the face of a negative emotion is to **S.T.O.P.**

S – Stop or pause (*Don't send that negative email or say something hurtful*)

T – Take a step back and breathe (*Walk away or put your phone down*)

O – Observe (*Notice your thoughts, feelings, emotions and physical sensations*)

P – Proceed mindfully (*Will this make it better or worse? Do nothing for now?*)

Choose your story

In the absence of information, we sometimes fill in the blanks with our own details. Perhaps you feel rejected because you haven't heard from a friend or loved one for a while, and the story you're telling yourself is that they don't care about you any more. To avoid falling into the emotional river, ask yourself what other explanations might be possible. What else might be happening in their life that has meant they haven't contacted you? Could they be busy, under pressure at home or work, or even be sick?

When drowning in your story of blaming others, another helpful technique is to add 'just like me' to the end of every negative comment you tell yourself about that person. For example, 'This person wants to be seen and heard, just like me.' Doing this reinforces your ability to become more empathetic, compassionate and kind, and **choose** a better story.

Choose how you're going to respond

As Jocko Willink, former US Navy SEAL and author of *Extreme Ownership: How US Navy SEALs Lead and Win*, advises, when facing a challenge, 'Relax. Look around. Make a call.' In most situations, you have a **choice** about how to respond. If you tend to react in a knee-jerk manner to feelings of anger by lashing out at people, it's likely to mess up your relationships and communication with others. It may feel good now, but it won't over the long term as regret soon accumulates over time.

Next time you feel a powerful emotion, recognise that you can choose how to respond. Can you try a different response? Can you tell someone you're feeling angry rather than speaking to them harshly? Excuse yourself from the heated conversation and perhaps go for a walk. Get curious about what will happen if you switch up your responses.

Look for positive emotions

Human beings naturally attribute more weight to negative emotions than positive ones. But you need to be in a position where the opposite happens. The pleasant stuff sticks and the pain falls away. Negative emotions, such as disgust, envy and sadness, can feel heavy. Meanwhile, more positive feelings, like contentment, gratitude and flow, somehow feel lighter. Making a habit of noticing these positive experiences can boost your resilience and overall well-being.

HARNESS YOUR RED CENTRE

In the kidnap-for-ransom industry, particularly within law enforcement, the term Red Centre is ordinarily used to describe the epicentre of the negotiation, the physical location – usually a room in a house, hotel or office – where the family member or colleague of the hostage is receiving phone calls and demands from the kidnappers. It is a chaotic place, full of highly charged emotion, where people's lives hang in the balance.

However, the concept of a Red Centre is not just useful in hostage negotiation. It's a place deep within you that you can tap into when faced with unexpected or unpleasant situations. It is also a place where you can strip back the fear and unhelpful conditioning built up over a lifetime that gets in the way of achieving your full potential.

Each day I was on a case, I would wake up and take a reading of how I was feeling by tuning into my in-built emotional barometer, my Red Centre. When I was deployed on the ground in-country, rather than remotely managing the situation over the phone from thousands of miles away, doing this emotional check-in was even more important.

You may not be negotiating with kidnappers, but using the techniques described in this book to create your own Red Centre will reap rewards for your personal and professional life. A Red Centre will enable you to meet adversity head-on and think, decide, and act far more effectively than before. It will help you to crush that important business deal, study for a degree while holding down two jobs, run your first ten-kilometre race, lose stubborn post-holiday weight or achieve that long-held dream, whatever that might be for you.

These inner resources are the strengths and skills that help you deal with whatever life throws your way. This well of resourcefulness enables you to trust that you'll always find a way to overcome. Consider the Red Centre concept as a sanctuary or stronghold representing a state of inner resilience, strength and tranquillity in this fast-paced world. By cultivating self-awareness, rationality and acceptance of things beyond your control, the Red Centre remains impenetrable to external disturbances, such as adversity, temptation or criticism.

See it also as a state of mental resilience and strength where your thoughts, emotions and judgements are under your control and unaffected by the chaos and turmoil of the outside world. Essentially, it's about cultivating a mental fortress – a place of inner strength and calm – enabling you to stand in the eye of the storm.

For example, you might face a tough day at work with multiple deadlines and demanding clients. Instead of letting stress overwhelm you, tap into your Red Centre and practise mindfulness to stay present, maintain perspective on the situation and respond with clarity rather than reacting impulsively. This allows you to tackle each task with focus and efficiency, ultimately achieving better outcomes.

Similarly, consider a situation where you face criticism or negativity on social media. Rather than letting it affect your self-esteem or mood, you draw upon your Red Centre, practising self-awareness, compassion and emotional resilience. This lets you recognise that your true value lies within, independent of external validation or approval from others.

Exercise

One way you can manage your emotional state and harness your Red Centre is by using this simple three-step process, which will enable you to take everything in your stride, specifically in moments of uncertainty and confusion.

It will also help you to make effective decisions, whether you're leading others or dealing with something on your own, such as facing a relationship challenge or competing demands on your time.

Firstly, **acknowledge** and **accept** where you find yourself in that very moment. Take ownership.

The second step is to **locate** where in your body you are

experiencing the tension, tightness or some other uncomfortable feeling.

Thirdly, **breathe** through that sensation, sitting with it, not forcing it away or allowing yourself to be consumed by it. Step into it, see, feel and experience it, until it begins to dissipate.

Once you've taken these steps, begin to **clarify** what triggered you in the first place. Consider what it is that you need to be able to operate, interact and decide from a place of strength, rather than with an ill-considered reaction or opinion.

By moving through these stages, you'll begin to embody feelings of calmness, highly tuned intuition and presence, which will allow you to think more clearly and act in a way that leads to a positive outcome.

FOCUS ON THE TRIGGERS

'Nothing ever goes away until it has taught us what we need to know.'

Pema Chodron

We hear so much these days about how people are 'triggered' or have had their buttons pressed by what someone has said or done, or not said or done, and somehow it's the other person's fault. They have offended you as if you were the most fragile thing in the world. The reality is that the actual trigger usually doesn't warrant such an excessive reaction.

The word 'trigger' comes from the Dutch word 'pull'. When triggered, you are pulled into an emotive reaction, and your rational side is taken hostage and tricked. As writer and psychotherapist David Richo says, 'You're being bullied by your own unfinished business.'

Triggers activate the 'sympathetic' part of your autonomic nervous system, which helps activate your fight, flight or freeze response. All is not lost, though. The extent of your reaction is based mainly on your beliefs about the other person or situation, and the meaning you ascribe to events and actions. It fires off an immediate reaction in your limbic system, where your emotions reside. However, you have the agency to train your pre-frontal cortex to reframe and reprogramme your neurological and emotional patterns and give new, more empowering meaning to your experiences.

Another factor to consider is that when we are triggered or disturbed by others, it is often because they reflect parts of ourselves, perhaps our fears, insecurities or unresolved issues. This is an opportunity for us to grow and understand ourselves better. By recognising this, we can transform difficult interactions into powerful lessons for self-awareness and healing.

For example, someone on your team always seems to annoy you because they never meet deadlines. Every time they miss one, you feel frustrated and get stressed out. By seeing this person as a reflection of something that needs resolving within you, you have an opportunity to reflect on why their behaviour affects you so strongly. When you sit down and give it some thought, it slowly begins to dawn on you that perhaps their tardiness triggers your own fear of being seen as unreliable or unprofessional, or perhaps it highlights your struggle with perfectionism and control.

Another time you get fed up with a colleague who always seems to interrupt you during meetings, which you find rude and disrespectful. If you focus on what it is that triggers you, it might tell you that your irritation stems from your own insecurities about being heard or valued in group settings. Perhaps you've always had a fear of not being taken seriously, and this person's behaviour is triggering that unresolved fear. So, instead of focusing on how the colleague is 'rude', you could use the experience to better understand your sensitivity around feeling ignored. It becomes an opportunity for personal growth, allowing you to address your own insecurities, develop confidence and communicate more assertively.

When someone inflicts physical violence upon you, it can trigger fear, helplessness or anger. This is due to the perpetrator's actions. But when you're not in immediate physical danger, it's up to you to work out what the trigger is. David Richo reminds us: 'Being triggered is not dysfunctional, but your reaction to a trigger might be.' If you can develop a more conscious, focused awareness, this new pathway becomes the norm over time, enabling you to deactivate the trigger.

Developing a thicker skin means you become more resilient and less sensitive to negative experiences, criticisms or setbacks in life, such as a relationship breakup, bad weather on your special day or travel disruption en route to an important meeting.

One way to develop this is to stay curious about why certain things bother you. Instead of running away from them, you face them head-on and learn from them. You also avoid letting yourself feel powerless or controlled by someone else's words or actions, using those moments as signals to explore what's going on inside you. Investigating your reactions can uncover many unresolved issues or insecurities contributing to your sensitivity. It's like seeing a trigger – a comment or event that bothers you – as a sign that you might need to understand or work through something deeper. Examine why it bothered you and made you feel the way it did, rather than being easily offended or annoyed. Doing so will help you to become stronger and more resilient in the face of life's challenges and criticisms, allowing you to engage with the world more confidently and cope with whatever comes your way.

CASE STUDY #2

Anger is one of the key emotions that all humans experience right from birth.[*]

Levels of anger tend to peak in early childhood and reduce as children become more socialised and better able to control their emotions. Of course, anger is a normal feeling: we all experience it occasionally. However, the problem arises when anger remains an issue long after others have learned to control it.

According to the British Association of Anger Management, 80 per cent of people believe Britain is becoming angrier. Britain is also ranked highest in road-rage incidents in Europe.

John, a 35-year-old software engineer, was well known for his technical skills and problem-solving abilities at work. However, behind his professional image, John struggled with intense frustration and anger, leading to frequent outbursts and strained relationships both at work and home.

Growing up in a household where emotions were suppressed and conflict was avoided, John learned to bury his feelings. However, as work and personal life pressures increased, John found it harder to control his temper. Small frustrations quickly turned into sudden fits of rage, leaving John feeling ashamed and isolated.

Realising the impact this was having on his relationships and state of mind, John took ownership and decided to manage how he reacted to his triggers. He did this by noticing whenever negative thought patterns would show up, such as catastrophising – 'If this project fails, I won't get promoted and it'll ruin my career.' He was then able to recognise the warning signs and utilise healthy coping strategies, such as breathing exercises and reframing to calm down before it got worse.

[*] https://cpdonline.co.uk/knowledge-base/mental-health/anger-management-programmes/

Over time, John's new behaviour had a positive ripple effect on his relationships at work and home, eventually breaking the cycle.

SUMMARY

Science shows that your emotions are made and not triggered. What does this mean? It means you must take 100 per cent responsibility and ownership for how you feel at any given moment, regardless of the situation or circumstances. You can't outsource it to someone else – in other words, you can't blame, name or shame someone or something else for how you feel. This doesn't mean you condone, accept or acquiesce to what has happened; but you must admit that how you feel is down to you. How does this help you? Well, it gives you tremendous freedom and agency to live on your terms rather than delegating it to things you can't control.

We are also responsible for how we behave in response to those emotions, including doing something to positively change them. Remember, emotions have no moral status. They are passive experiences, whereas your actions are your choices.

As we've already explored in this chapter, emotions are not inherently good or bad. They can be viewed as being natural, automatic reactions to circumstances, determined by your biology, psychology and personal experience, rather than a conscious choice based on a judgement.

For instance, feeling anger, frustration or jealousy is often (but not always) seen as a spontaneous, uncontrollable human reaction to perceived threats, injustice, or expectations not being met, rather than some deliberate moral failing. Whether you express these feelings peacefully or by harming someone or damaging something is completely down to you. Conversely, feeling an emotion such as joy is not inherently virtuous either; it is the way in which joy might lead to positive or negative behaviours that is important.

If you separate how you feel from your subsequent behaviour, you can be compassionate towards yourself and others. You can acknowledge that you cannot always control what you feel (at least not initially), but you can absolutely exercise control over how you respond to those feelings, as we'll discover later in this book.

By viewing your emotions in this way, you will begin to release any sense of guilt or shame you feel about having certain feelings. Your focus may be better spent on how you recognise, manage and express them without judgement, yet with appropriate sensitivity to their possible impact on others. At the same time, you can practise cultivating self-awareness, emotional regulation and ethical decision-making based on the meaning you choose to give emotions and the actions you take as a result.

KEY TAKEAWAYS

1. Emotional self-regulation is the #1 skill you can learn.
2. Separate your emotions from your thoughts (you're in charge).
3. Emotions drive everything (but they have no moral status).

5

Emotional Tolerance

'The most important single ingredient in the formula of success is knowing how to get along with people, (including ourselves).'

Theodore Roosevelt

What we'll cover:

- **Chronic stress and how to overcome it**
- **Distress tolerance and how to increase it**
- **Emotional vampires and how to deal with them**

In the previous chapter, you learned how emotions, while not inherently good or bad, impact you based on various factors such as your biology, psychology and personal experience. You also learned how to regulate your emotions, so you start taking back control of how you think, feel and act.

This chapter explores the most common ways you might find yourself under duress and experiencing what is called an 'emotional hijack'. This is usually when you say or do something you later regret. We'll also cover what you can do to prevent it from happening, and, if it does, how you can recover from it more easily.

One way you might find yourself being hijacked like this is as a result of encounters with a certain type of individual. This type of person is someone you've likely encountered and had to deal with many times at work and possibly even closer to home. These people are best described as 'emotional vampires'. As their name suggests, they are all about themselves and will drain the positive energy from you, often leaving you feeling worse after interacting with them.

CASE STUDY #1

Sarah, a 35-year-old office manager and mother of two, has a busy full-time job for a large professional services firm. A fifty-plus-hour working week is not uncommon for her. She'll often jump on her laptop and continue working late into the evening after her young kids are in bed. Despite this workload, Sarah is well organised, upbeat and able to handle the normal ups and downs of life and manage both her personal life and work reasonably well.

Over the last few months, however, things have changed. Sarah's workload and responsibilities have increased following the arrival of her new, ambitious and demanding boss, who is keen to make a name for himself. At home, one of her children has also started having trouble in school, and with her husband's business losing a major client recently, the family's finances have also grown tight.

These constant worries and demands on her attention, energy and time are beginning to take their toll on her emotions and ability to make clear, rational decisions. As the stress continues to build, Sarah starts feeling overwhelmed more frequently.

This is not surprising as she is no longer creating space to relax, recharge or enjoy herself.

At work, her once-clear thinking has become clouded. Instead of confidently moving forward with projects, she has become increasingly indecisive. Recently, she spent hours reviewing a report she would normally have understood easily, fearing she had missed important details. It's not like her to be uncertain, but the stress makes her feel as if she can't trust her own judgement. She's also snapped a couple of times at a younger colleague for minor mistakes.

At home, things aren't getting any better. After a long day at work, Sarah feels physically and mentally exhausted. She becomes irritable with the kids, and even simple tasks like helping them with homework feel too much. One evening, her daughter asks for help with a maths problem, but Sarah, feeling overwhelmed, shouts at her to figure it out on her own. Afterwards, she feels guilty for her overreaction.

This pattern continues for weeks. Sarah notices that her patience is wearing thin in nearly every area of her life. She becomes more irritable with her family and withdrawn from her friends, even though she knows they can offer support. She also finds herself cancelling social plans because she feels she can't handle one more thing on her plate. Over time, this isolation deepens her stress, and she finds herself feeling increasingly anxious and alone. Her sleep is suffering, too, as she's often lying awake at night thinking about her endless to-do list. The chronic stress she's under is taking a massive toll on both her body and her mind.

This ongoing chronic stress has caused her body to be stuck in a hypervigilant state fuelled by continuously elevated levels of cortisol and adrenaline. These hormones can be helpful in short bursts because so-called 'good stress' motivates us, and helps us to meet deadlines and solve problems; prolonged exposure to it keeps Sarah's body in a constant state of high alert. This makes it harder for her to relax, focus and make rational decisions. This is why Sarah is feeling so indecisive and irritable.

Left unchecked, chronic stress like Sarah's can lead to emotional exhaustion, decision fatigue and burnout that can take months or years to recover from. Recognising the signs and taking steps to manage it, such as seeking support, practising mindfulness or setting boundaries, can help restore balance and clarity in our lives. Over time, this is exactly what Sarah did and gradually learned how to manage her stress better, which enabled her to return to the confident, clear-headed person she used to be. We'll explore how you can tackle chronic stress later in the chapter.

I'm sure most of us know someone like Sarah or can at least relate to some of the challenges ourselves. Her situation shows how chronic stress can affect everyday life, leading to emotional burnout, poor decision-making and strained relationships. In other words, a pretty miserable life.

Before we get to that, let's look at the impact stress, and particularly chronic stress, can have on your emotions, which in turn impacts how you think when faced with difficult people or situations.

CHRONIC STRESS AND HOW TO OVERCOME IT

To begin with, we need to understand the difference between acute and chronic stress.

ACUTE STRESS
- **Duration**: Short-term, immediate response to a specific situation.

- **Causes**: Events or situations that are new, unpredictable or pose a perceived threat. Examples include you taking a test, giving a presentation or suddenly finding yourself in an argument.
- **Physical response**: Activates the body's fight, flight or freeze response, leading to increased heart rate, breathing, heightened alertness and the release of hormones such as adrenaline and cortisol.
- **Effect on health**: While it can be intense, acute stress is usually temporary and can sometimes be beneficial by helping you to focus and react quickly. However, frequent bouts of acute stress can lead to issues such as headaches, digestive problems or muscle tension.
- **Recovery**: Your body usually returns to a healthy baseline state relatively quickly once the stressor is gone.

CHRONIC STRESS
- **Duration**: Long-term and persistent.
- **Causes**: Ongoing and unresolved situations or circumstances such as financial difficulties, a challenging job, relationship problems or chronic illness.
- **Physical response**: Keeps the body in a prolonged state of stress, with adrenaline and cortisol continuously affecting the body resulting in a dysregulated and unbalanced nervous system.
- **Effect on health**: Serious health issues like heart disease, high blood pressure, depression, anxiety, weakened immune function and sleep problems.
- **Recovery**: More difficult to resolve, as often requires addressing the root cause of the stress and may require lifestyle changes or professional intervention.

In summary, acute stress is short-lived and linked to specific events, while chronic stress is long-term and more damaging to overall health.

Your autonomic nervous system has two components: the sympathetic and the parasympathetic. We can think of the sympathetic as the accelerator and the parasympathetic as the brake pedal. Under normal conditions, such as when you're exercising or recovering from an injury or illness, your sympathetic nervous system increases the amount of oxygenated blood pumping around your body, helping it to recover and repair naturally.

However, if you're constantly stimulated and stressed from repetitive, prolonged and intense situations, just like we saw with Sarah in the previous case study, the gas pedal is always pressed down, and you're forever accelerating in fight or flight mode. This can lead to a litany of health issues, including anxiety, high blood pressure, chronic fatigue syndrome, heart attacks and more.

Although your body sends clear signals when you need a break, such as fidgetiness, hunger, drowsiness or a loss of focus, you probably tend to override them by finding artificial ways to increase your energy, such as excessive caffeine, sugary foods, simple carbohydrates and dopamine hits from scrolling aimlessly on social media.

The following diagram shows the impact stress and certain emotions can have on your body if left unchecked.

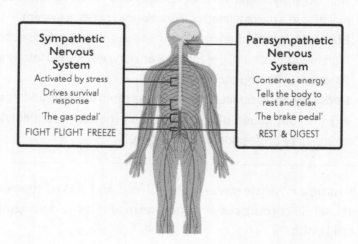

Learning to use the brake pedal a little more will allow your body to 'rest and digest'. When the parasympathetic nervous system is activated, your heart and breathing rates slow, and your blood pressure reduces. Your body enters a state of relaxation, which in turn supports recovery. The quicker you can return to this state, the healthier you become. It also enables you to develop a tolerance to stress and an agency to deal more effectively when facing life's challenges.

How do you achieve this?

You can activate your parasympathetic nervous system in many ways, and it's important to find whichever works best for you. Consistency is key. These include breathing exercises, relaxing music, spending time in nature, playing with a pet, sunlight exposure, journalling, meditation, painting, reading, yoga and much more.

Exercise

One way to activate your parasympathetic nervous system is to regularly practise Non-Sleep Deep Rest (NSDR). This is a deep relaxation method developed by Dr Andrew Huberman, a neuro-scientist and professor at Stanford University School of Medicine, and it is based on the traditional practice of Yoga Nidra.

In a ten- or twenty-minute guided meditation, NSDR combines mindful breathing and body scanning to make you fully aware yet completely relaxed. This proven exercise resets and balances your nervous system, increasing your energy levels and cognitive performance, improving your sleep and overall well-being. Ultimately, it will make it easier for you to deal with adversity.

How does it work? As your body becomes calmer and slows the production of cortisol, your parasympathetic nervous system kicks into gear.

To practise NSDR, follow these seven steps:

1. **Find a quiet and comfortable space**
Choose a peaceful environment without any distractions. Switch off all notifications on your devices.

2. **Get into a comfortable position**
Lie down on your back or sit comfortably on a chair, with your arms relaxed by your sides.

3. **Follow a guided NSDR recording**
Various guided audio recordings are available online, such as https://go.hubermanlab.com/10-min-nsdr. Find a reliable source whose voice and guidance resonates with you. Use these recordings to help you navigate the practice.

4. **Relax your body**
Once you have begun, focus on relaxing your body and releasing tension. The guided recording will lead you by focusing on different body parts, bringing awareness to each area before consciously relaxing it.

5. **Breathe and visualise**
Observe your breath, ideally breathing through your nose and out through your mouth using thinly pursed lips as if you were blowing through a straw. As you do so, you'll be asked to imagine different scenes or sensations that promote relaxation and calmness. Allow yourself to experience the guided imagery fully.

6. **Maintain awareness and stay present**
Throughout the practice, remain aware and present. Although deep relaxation is induced (and can sometimes result in you falling asleep), it is important to maintain a

subtle level of consciousness where possible, observing any
sensations, thoughts or emotions that arise.

7. **Conclude the practice**
The guided recording will eventually guide you back to a state
of wakefulness. Take your time to transition, slowly bringing
your awareness to the present moment. Reflect on your experience and any insights you may have gained.

Another way to ensure you can remain in a balanced state is to
routinise your day as much as possible. For example, after
you've worked at a high intensity or on deep work for more
than ninety minutes, you may lose focus and move from parasympathetic to sympathetic arousal (it's the old 'fight or flight'
again).

Relying on stress hormones for energy also has a consequence: the pre-frontal cortex (the part of the brain that regu-
lates your thoughts, actions and emotions) begins to shut down.
As a result, you'll become more reactive and lose the capability
to think clearly and reflectively or see the bigger picture.
Consider the following to help you stay as focused as possible
for longer.

Action:
Identify two or three ninety-minute periods of your day –
otherwise known as ultradian cycles – where you can properly
focus and engage in your most meaningful and important
tasks. After each one, consider taking a break from screens or
other stimulation to enable your nervous system to reset before
engaging in the next cycle.

Most high performers usually have no more than three such
cycles each day despite the pressure to do more. They have
discovered the ability to be laser-focused and apply themselves

in a concentrated way on the things that really matter, rather than the noise of inconsequential and irrelevant stuff.

DISTRESS TOLERANCE AND HOW TO INCREASE IT

Distress tolerance is your ability to tolerate uncomfortable emotions, sensations and experiences, that you can often do nothing about. It enables you to withstand emotional distress – in other words, being comfortable with being uncomfortable. To do so effectively and consistently is a hallmark of mental well-being. This can't be achieved by reading a book, listening to a podcast or wearing a T-shirt with #resilience emblazoned across the front; it must be practised and experienced repeatedly.

Emotional *dys*regulation often comes from your desire to override an uncomfortable or painful feeling. Rather than expanding awareness and developing resilience, people often look to escape this stress through maladaptive and impulsive behaviours, such as consuming excessive amounts of alcohol or recreational drugs, binge eating, engaging in reckless sexual behaviour, or, in severe cases, self-harm. Your behaviour doesn't have to be this extreme, though. Most of us might seek to escape by scrolling on social media or biting our nails. With practice, you can learn how to calm yourself down in more helpful and sustainable ways, and take life's challenges in your stride.

Some people are better at regulating their emotions than others. They are high in emotional intelligence and are aware of their internal experiences and the feelings of others. While it may seem like they're just naturally calm, these people experience negative feelings, too. They've just developed coping strategies that allow them to become comfortable with discomfort and powerful emotions, which we can all learn and master over time. As we now know, learning how to manage negative experiences can benefit your overall mental and physical health.

For some people, it's not that easy to do. Particularly if they are experiencing feelings of abandonment or of not belonging; for them, when someone they trust doesn't follow through on a promise or a relationship ends, it can feel like the end of world and that the pain will last for ever.

Let's look at some ways in which you can increase your distress tolerance. It might be that you can resolve the situation you find yourself in (without making it worse), which means you can then move on. Doing this will obviously build your ability to manage your emotions, make effective decisions and take appropriate action.

However, sometimes you might be in a situation that feels all-consuming, and you need to alleviate it but can't because of other constraints. For example, there might be repercussions if you tell your boss what you really think of. You might deliberately choose to distract yourself for a short while to allow tempers to cool, perhaps by going for a swim or to a gym class to avoid having a row with your partner.

Pushing problems and emotions away is usually not a good idea as they can fester and come back even worse. Sometimes though, asking yourself, 'Can I actually do anything about this right now?' or 'Am I in the best frame of mind to deal with this?' can help you park the issue with an acknowledgement that you will come back and deal with it at a more appropriate time.

I experienced this multiple times as a police detective and

later in my career when I was engaged in negotiations. I couldn't afford to allow whatever issues I had going on in my own life at that time to get in the way of me completely focusing on supporting distraught families, whose loved one had been the victim of a serious crime or taken hostage. While distracting or 'parking it' doesn't solve the problem, it does create an invaluable pause, allowing your emotions to subside before addressing the issue.

Engaging in radical acceptance is also essential for building distress tolerance. This means accepting a situation as it is, even if it's painful.

EMOTIONAL VAMPIRES AND HOW TO DEAL WITH THEM

'No one can make you feel inferior without your consent.'
                                                Eleanor Roosevelt

Emotional vampires are everywhere. Chances are you know a colleague, client, friend or family member who can drain you emotionally through their constant negativity, manipulation or self-centred behaviour. Hurt people hurt other people, and emotional vampires have been hurt previously, often extensively. There always seems to be some drama or crisis in their lives. And it's never their fault because they're the victims. Every. Single. Time. They swing between delusions of grandeur at one end and deep victimhood and catastrophising at the other, as well as often coming across as 'needy'. Sound familiar? If you allow them to, they can ruin your life.

Research shows emotional vampires thrive in the workplace because many of us link our identities to what we do for a living.

We bring our whole selves to our jobs and measure our self-worth against our accomplishments. Unsurprisingly, emotional vampires feed on what you care about most. How do they do this? By gaslighting, manipulating or using other emotionally controlling tactics to weaken others. Whether they do this intentionally or not, they often leave others feeling depressed, anxious and insecure.

They may or may not be aware of their behaviour, but their desire to distract from their insecurities doesn't make their behaviours any less toxic. They ensure they're never at fault by controlling the narrative, particularly as they avoid taking responsibility or ownership for their actions or lives. They keep themselves firmly at the centre, winning a gold medal for victimhood in the process.

While they may not drink blood, they can still drain the well-being, vitality and confidence from those around them. Fortunately, just like their fictional counterparts, turning a bright light on their behaviour is an excellent way of keeping them at bay.

Types of emotional vampires and how to spot them:

Narcissist

Narcissists seem unable to talk about anything but themselves. Even if you are upset or going through something difficult, they still can't take their attention off themselves long enough to empathise. It is challenging when you have a close personal relationship with them as we rely on the people closest to us to help us navigate difficult times. Narcissists are too emotionally immature and self-centred to see when you need help; 'Are you done whining yet? I haven't even told you what happened to me', 'That's nothing; at least you're not dealing with what I'm dealing with.'

Drama lover

This type always seems to be dealing with an emotional crisis of one sort or another. If something is going well for them, they'll minimise it or still find something to complain about. If something isn't going that well, be prepared to hear all about it for a long time. It's as if their dramatic story is playing on a never-ending loop, with it being retold at every opportunity they get. Nor does the setback have to be significant, as they can find a way to turn almost anything into a catastrophic story; 'I guess I'm excited about my promotion, but I'll just be in a higher tax bracket now', 'How am I? What's the last thing I told you? Things have gotten even worse.'

Victim

Nothing is ever the victim's fault. Even when you have 'hard evidence', they'll do some impressive emotional and mental acrobatics to justify their behaviour. These people are very sensitive to perceived criticism and will lash out if you try to point out what they could have done differently. You'll also find that they don't take advice well and seem uninterested in problem-solving. They always have a reason why it won't work, so they see little point in trying. They'd much rather wallow in a draining, self-pitying mindset often used to manipulate others or deflect responsibility; 'Are you blaming me? If they had done their part, I would have finished my bit on time!', 'I'd help you out, but no one ever helps me when I need it. So, why should I bother?', 'Nothing ever goes right for me, no matter how hard I work at it.'

People with a victim mentality are often more interested in pity, sympathy or attention rather than solutions. In other words, they've mastered learned helplessness, where they gain significance by playing the role of victim as it feeds into their sense of identity. They blame others or situations – often from a long time ago – for their current feelings or life conditions today. The reality is that they have complete agency to move on from it, taking ownership and responsibility for what they do next, yet they choose not to.

Entitled

This emotional vampire is a close relative of the 'victim', and one that is rapidly multiplying today. They can usually be found immersed in one of many contentious topics such as gender, climate, race, politics, etc., and be heard shouting the loudest, so as not to allow any alternative voice to be heard. They firmly believe that they have an entitlement (based solely on their opinion) to force every other person to adhere to and adopt their point of view. They are right, and if you don't agree with them, you are wrong. And woe betide if you don't blindly acquiesce and fall into line with them because they're usually quick to shout, ostracise, vilify, cancel and de-platform; 'I find it offensive that anyone could think differently on this topic', 'We need to shut down these harmful ideas before they spread', or 'If you don't agree with us on this, you're part of the problem.'

This entitled mentality insists on absolute adherence to a specific belief, and attempts to control or silence all opposing views, usually by shutting down any form of dialogue with those who may disagree with them. Attention is like oxygen for such vampires; therefore, they're best ignored, which is what most people do anyway.

Controller

Similar in many ways to the 'entitled', but you're less likely to find 'controllers' protesting, as they're more likely to be leading others in a corporate or organisational environment, usually in the guise of the classic micro-manager.

If you find yourself talking to someone who makes you feel like there's only one right answer, you're probably talking to a controlling person. This is not the same as someone who may have a difference of opinion to yours – that's healthy. It's when they often make you feel like you must get their approval on absolutely everything, even though you have the skills, experience or authority to make your own decisions. They can be domineering or subtle in their manipulations. After talking to someone controlling, you often feel like you're second-guessing yourself; 'You really should have talked to me about that first.'

Talker

Excessively talkative people may dominate the conversation with their own opinions and views. If you do get a chance to speak up, they quickly dismiss you to get back to what they were saying. You may bump into these types of vampires while out and about. They'll spend ages updating you on their life and at no point will they ask questions about you or display any interest whatsoever about how things were going with your new dog/cat/child/job/car/husband/wife/lover/haircut, etc.

These people always think about what they'll say next while you're talking – if you even get chance to talk, that is. If you call them out on it, they can often recite what you said but miss the nuance of it. Talkers find a way to spin everything back to their original point. They can't deal with silence; 'That reminds me – I have to tell you about what happened to me', 'You're always interrupting me. You don't listen to anyone but yourself.'

Here are some toxic behaviours that emotional vampires commonly display:

Gaslighting

Gaslighting is a way of making you doubt your own sanity, perception of reality or instincts. Whether conscious or unconscious, a gaslighter can make you feel like you don't know what you're talking about and even make you doubt your own memory.

Passive-aggressive behaviour

People who are passive-aggressive will rarely ask for what they want. Instead, they try to manipulate you into doing what they want you to do. They will often hold you accountable for not meeting their expectations, even if they were never communicated properly.

No accountability

Emotional vampires rarely take responsibility for their actions. If you point out a mistake they've made or an action they took that hurt you, they'll often find a way to blame it on you – or, at least, anyone but themselves.

Guilt

Guilt is a favourite weapon of emotional vampires. Once they make you feel guilty, they keep going until you feel the need to apologise. They often use it as a way out of taking any responsibility themselves.

All-or-nothing thinking

Lots of people tend towards all-or-nothing patterns. It's a common feature of mood disorders like anxiety and depression. That alone doesn't make them emotional vampires. However, it can become toxic when people apply their all-or-nothing thoughts to others. They may describe people as either good or bad, hard-working or lazy, smart or stupid. At best, this is reductive; at worst, it's damaging.

Makes inappropriate or personal comments

Emotional vampires frequently get too close too fast. Sometimes, this is a tactic to uncover sensitive or personal information that can be used to manipulate you. Asking personal questions can also subtly shift power away from you by putting you on your guard.

'All about me' syndrome

This often shows up as self-centred or egocentric behaviour. There's no use in trying to tell them about something that happened to you. They're wholly uninterested unless it has something to do with them. And they'll always find a way to connect everything back to themselves.

Your own feelings

By far one of the most important indicators of an emotional vampire is how you feel after you interact with them – especially over an extended period. If you feel emotionally exhausted, depressed, insecure or wish that you had never said anything at all, that person is probably an emotional vampire.

It's a fact of life that you have to deal with people you don't like or get on with. Even if you don't enjoy their presence, you still need to learn to collaborate and communicate effectively with them. While we can't control when and how emotional vampires appear, we can limit their impact on us. Developing strategies to deal with toxic people and their behaviours in your life can help you feel more in control. You'll be less stressed, have more energy and develop resilience, along with strategies to handle such behaviour.

Here are five steps to deal with an emotional vampire:

Step 1. Set clear boundaries
Emotional vampires love to live in the grey areas. The less clarity there is, the more they can get away with. Hold them accountable for their actions. Set clear boundaries for their behaviour with you and your expectations of them. For example, if you're dealing with someone who is chronically late, get the time that you're supposed to meet them in writing. Make it clear that if they're not there after fifteen minutes, you're leaving – and follow through if they're late. Setting boundaries helps you limit the negative impact of their behaviour on you. When the consequences of their behaviour begin to affect them instead, they'll be motivated to change.

Step 2. Stick to the facts
Emotional vampires are called that for a reason. They love to manipulate you through your feelings. Stick to the facts when dealing with these people. Instead of telling them how they made you feel, give them examples of specific behaviours that need to change. For example, if you're dealing with a victim vampire, you can say, 'I'm sorry that you're dealing with this, but I'm unwilling to . . . [insert boundary here].' If it's happening at work, talk to a manager or encourage the vampire to take their concerns to HR.

Step 3. Practise mindfulness

One of the best ways to limit the impact of emotional vampires is to develop self-awareness of how their behaviours affect you. Practising mindfulness can help you become aware of which emotional strings they're pulling to manipulate you and why it affects you. Mindfulness practices can help you avoid being triggered or pulled into a game of blaming, naming or shaming.

Step 4. Talk to a therapist or coach

Emotional vampires – especially when they're family members or loved ones – can do real damage to our mental health. When someone you trust or love makes you feel put down, it hurts your self-esteem and trust and drains your emotional energy. Relationships with energy vampires are often co-dependent and stressful.

Working with a professional can be helpful when it comes to setting boundaries and taking an objective look at the relationship. This kind of work can help you identify patterns, improve low self-esteem and sort out your emotional reactions. Sometimes, toxic traits are a sign of a personality disorder or a precursor to emotional and mental abuse.

Step 5. Interact virtually (or not at all)

Can't get away from them at work or elsewhere? Keep them at a distance. While you may not have control over where they work or how they're related to you, you can have some control over how you interact with them. Drawing a line where you interact, or if you even engage face to face in the first place, can restore some of your emotional freedom. Protecting your mental health is a good reason to turn a meeting with an emotional vampire into an email instead.

CASE STUDY #2

Emotions often run high in the workplace. Employees are constantly faced with stressors such as tight deadlines, challenging colleagues and demanding clients. These can all threaten to derail productivity and well-being. This is where emotional regulation comes into play. It's a crucial skill that can make all the difference between a supportive, thriving workplace and one fraught with tension and conflict.

At Company A, a fast-paced tech start-up known for its innovative products and cutting-edge solutions, emotions often run high due to tight deadlines and expectations. While the company's rapid growth has inspired excitement and ambition, it has also created an environment where stress and frustration are all too common. This pressure-cooker atmosphere has begun to affect team dynamics, with Mark and Emily emerging as disruptive forces.

While they are brilliant in their roles, they have both started to display the behaviours of emotional vampires, draining energy from others with their visible collusion, negativity and confrontational attitudes. Mark's constant criticism and refusal to collaborate creates tension, while Emily's passive-aggressive comments and unpredictable mood swings make it hard for her teammates to focus. Their unresolved personal conflict with others also threatens to spill over into the wider team, creating a toxic work environment.

Lisa, a talented software developer, and Steve, who is managing client relationships, bear the brunt of Mark and Emily's emotional drain. As their behaviours worsen, Lisa and Steve feel their energy and productivity slipping. Thankfully, they both recognise the importance of emotional regulation to protect their own well-being and maintain the team's performance.

Lisa, already overwhelmed with impending deadlines, decides to set firm boundaries. She limits her interactions with Mark and Emily, only engaging with them when absolutely necessary for the project. She also practises mindfulness techniques, taking regular breaks to clear her mind and regain focus. Instead of getting pulled into Mark and Emily's negativity loops, Lisa channels her energy into her tasks and staying calm.

Steve, facing a demanding client while trying to juggle this office drama, takes a similar approach. He practises active listening and empathy with the client, but when dealing with Mark and Emily, he uses assertive communication to reinforce his boundaries. Steve calmly reminds them of project priorities and redirects the conversation when they start to spiral into negativity or a victim mentality. By staying composed and professional, Steve avoids getting drawn into unnecessary conflicts and preserves his emotional energy.

Lisa and Steve's ability to manage their emotional vampire colleagues through emotional regulation, mindfulness and boundary setting allows them to lead by example, maintain a positive mindset and stay attentive to their work, not to mention preserving their sanity.

In high-pressure work environments like Company A, emotional regulation is not just a tool for managing personal stress, but a critical strategy for dealing with difficult personalities. Employees like Lisa and Steve thrive by cultivating self-awareness, resilience and firm boundaries, contributing to a healthier, more collaborative work culture.

SUMMARY

Humans are hardwired for connection. It's not in your nature to want to cut off relationships or dismiss the pain of others. But you can only help others when you're not depleted, and you certainly shouldn't do it at your own expense. That said, seeking out opportunities in your daily life to increase your distress tolerance can be helpful as it builds your resilience muscle, enabling you to take on and deal with challenges more easily, without them having such a negative impact on you. This holds true if you ensure you balance this by regulating your nervous system.

For the avoidance of doubt, distress tolerance isn't about avoiding or suppressing negative feelings; instead, it's about learning to manage them effectively. Recognising red flags in your relationships and prioritising self-care are also your most important weapons when dealing with emotional vampires.

KEY TAKEAWAYS

1. Chronic stress is a (literal) killer. Activate your parasympathetic nervous system by taking the time to 'rest and digest'.
2. Develop your emotional resilience by increasing your distress tolerance. Be comfortable with being uncomfortable.
3. Emotional vampires are a part of life. Practise mindfulness and set boundaries when dealing with them.

6

Emotional Mastery

'A loving person lives in a loving world. A hostile person lives in a hostile world. Everyone you meet is your mirror.'

Ken Keyes, Jr

What we'll cover:

- **Winning the emotional golden ticket**
- **How to stack the (emotional) odds in your favour**
- **Empathy is a doing word**

In the previous chapters, you learned how your emotions can impact your thoughts and behaviour, particularly when faced with life's challenges. You also discovered how to identify and deal with emotional vampires; those who lack self-awareness, require significant validation and attention, and are unwilling to accept responsibility when things go wrong.

This chapter builds on this foundation, and you'll learn how to stack the odds of succeeding, winning the emotional golden ticket and achieving emotional mastery. Why is this important?

Well, wouldn't you like to master your emotions no matter how much of a dick your boss is being, how much you dread facing that all-important business presentation or when your partner isn't understanding your point of view?

Before you can master your emotions, you must first recognise your hot buttons – those things that really trigger you. Emotions are contagious; if you're not careful, they can derail your communication with yourself and others. Once people get upset at one another, rational thinking goes out the window. Despite what you might believe, those pesky emotions are not the obstacle to dealing with and successfully overcoming difficult situations or a conversation with a loved one. Emotions are the very *means* of doing so. In my experience, the best communicators – and remember, you're communicating all day, every day even if you don't think you are – identify and influence their own and other's emotions instead of denouncing or ignoring them.

In this chapter, you'll learn a set of techniques and principles that will work immediately to help you develop your emotional mastery if you apply them consistently. Like all new skills, it might feel awkward initially, but the more you practise, the easier it gets and the more effective you become. This is Neuroplasticity 101. It's like cleaning your teeth with your non-dominant hand. It feels weird to begin with. But, over time, new neural pathways begin to form in your brain, and the more you do it, the stronger they become until it feels natural.

CASE STUDY #1

A couple of years ago, I was working a kidnapping case in Europe where we faced a daily onslaught of challenging conversations and unreasonable demand after demand. It was hard work, and we weren't making as much progress as needed. The longer this went on, the risk to the hostages only increased.

But these challenges weren't coming from the kidnappers, the so-called 'bad guys'. They were coming from our own side, specifically the executives from the company whose colleague, who I'll call Simon, had been taken while on a business development trip overseas. In comparison, negotiating with the kidnappers was relatively easy.

Meanwhile, the main point of contact for the company, I'll call him David, saw this as his moment to prove himself, perhaps with one eye on promotion. Our advice and recommendations on how to approach the negotiation – what to say, when, how and why – were ignored and dismissed without so much as a cursory acknowledgement. This was David's show, and he wanted to do it his way. We were just there to make up the numbers, or so it seemed.

The definition of insanity is often described as doing the same thing repeatedly and expecting different results. So, after a few weeks of making little progress with the kidnappers, let alone the client, it was decided we needed a different approach. This situation taught me never to be so fixed on your way of doing things that you miss other, more compelling ways of achieving your outcome.

Enough was enough. If David's attitude and behaviour didn't improve, it could negatively impact the welfare and safety of the hostage – something we couldn't afford to let happen. We needed to get David onside and to begin following our advice. This was a classic scenario of needing to influence someone we had no direct authority over. It was all about achieving cooperation, collaboration and, ultimately, some form of behavioural change.

Sitting down with him over coffee one morning before we switched on the phone to await the kidnapper's call, he and I had a conversation. It went along the following lines:

'It seems like you're frustrated with the lack of progress with the negotiations, David. Is it OK if I share with you where I think you're at with it all?' I began.

He nodded and I continued.

'It's important for you to have a hands-on approach so you feel like you can maximise the chances of getting Simon back. And, quite frankly, you don't trust anyone else around here to make the big calls.'

I stayed quiet and avoided the temptation to keep talking. I wanted silence to work its magic.

For what seemed like ages, but was probably only ten seconds, we both sat there, David looking off into the distance, me just marking time.

Eventually, David looked back over to me and slowly spoke, 'You could say that, yes.'

His response confirmed my initial impression that he was driven by the need to have certainty, be in control, receive external validation and not lose face in front of others. Now that I knew his inner drivers and human needs, I could communicate in a way that maximised the chances of him ceding some control and taking on board my advice.

But first, I needed to defuse the negative comment I was about to send his way.

'You're not going to like what I'm about to tell you. In fact, it's probably going to make you feel even more frustrated,' I said.

I sat there in stony silence once more. David looked at me with a quizzical, unsure look on his face, a sight that was now very familiar. Why did I do this? Because I wanted to forewarn him that I was about to say something likely to push his hot buttons. By me flagging it ahead of time, it defused the emotional charge and made it less likely that he'd shut down or, worse, fly off the handle.

I continued, 'You probably think I'm some outsider who thinks he can just fly in here and tell you, someone who's been here for years, what to do and how to do it.'

Again, I squeezed every last drop of benefit from the silence that had fallen on our conversation for as long as I could to let it sink in.

'Not quite. I'm just under pressure from all angles to get this resolved asap,' he said, shifting in his chair.

Sensing a tiny chink in his armour, I told him, 'I'm here to support and advise you as much or as little as you want me to. I'm not here to make decisions for you or the company. After all, you're the main guy in charge. It's what you do best. What I do know, is that there is a ninety-three per cent chance of this negotiation succeeding if we follow my advice.'

I continued. 'This approach has been tested and proven over many decades by many negotiators in many different countries. When you get Simon back, you can take full credit for it. If, for some reason, it doesn't work out, you can say you were simply taking expert advice, which ultimately proved to be wrong. You win either way.'

The hint of a smile emerged on David's face. 'I'm listening,' he said.

Three weeks later, David successfully negotiated Simon's release following the payment of a heavily reduced ransom.

WINNING THE EMOTIONAL GOLDEN TICKET

Remaining calm and focused while in the eye of a storm raging all around you involves you simply having better conversations with those you're communicating with, whether it's your colleagues, clients, spouse, kids or, most importantly, yourself. People usually become nervous or avoid such conversations completely. At one end, you have people who believe they're some hot-shot negotiator who likes to play hardball. At the other, people are paralysed with fear when they're faced with having to persuade others to give them something, and so they cave in too easily, often walking away worse off as a result.

This is often due to the latter type of person overthinking what we mean when we use the term negotiation. A negotiation is simply a conversation with a purpose. It applies whether you're trying to attract investment capital for your business, deciding where to go on holiday with your partner or trying to get your kids to bed on time. It also applies to a conversation you have with yourself about whether you should take that new job, end a relationship or respond to whatever curveball has been thrown at you. Life is a negotiation and it's driven by one thing. Emotion.

Why is it worth winning?

Imagine you could peer inside another person's head while communicating with them. Once you've taken a rummage around inside, you know exactly which parts of their brain to stimulate so you can influence and persuade them to cooperate with you or change how they feel. Imagine being able to do this for yourself. This is what we mean by winning the emotional golden ticket. And it works with everyone.

Sounds devilishly Machiavellian, doesn't it? But it's far from that, because your intention matters. If you intend to manipulate and coerce others, you'll undoubtedly be labelled as some aspiring or actual narcissist or sociopath. Whereas, if you genuinely intend to understand how the other person sees the issue or situation and then take steps to reflect your understanding back to them, ultimately seeking some form of collaboration or cooperation built on mutual trust, you'll have yourself a client or partner for life.

Why is this? Because every single decision you make is to experience a particular emotion. For example, you want to drive a sports car, earn millions or get a promotion at work. I'm going to take a wild guess here, but I reckon it's not to own a piece of metal and rubber with a fancy badge stuck on it, or a million pieces of paper with pictures of dead people on them, or just some random letters formed together to make a 'job title'.

It'll be the feeling of driving your new car fast with the wind in your hair or the sensation in your stomach as your foot presses the accelerator further down into the floor. It's the feel-good sensation that comes with having a life-changing amount of money. It's the new sense of identity and belief that this promotion gives you. All of them are, first and foremost, emotionally driven.

Remember, we're feeling creatures that think, not thinking creatures that feel. Our subconscious drives us, forming learned responses to our experiences over many years. This, in turn, creates a blueprint for interpreting the world around us.

As a negotiator, I know that most kidnappers are just businessmen looking for the best deal. They're not rational people – but neither are you or I. They care about the same things we all do – not just getting the ransom but also power, control, respect and saving face. When our deeply held beliefs or position are challenged (even if we know we might be in the wrong), it can prove an existential threat to our sense of identity.

Each one of these factors can stir up strong emotions. Ignoring or failing to understand the emotions present in a conversation will derail it. Identifying and influencing them will only increase your chances of success.

Surely, when we're having a difficult conversation or are in a business negotiation, can't we just list some pros and cons for our options, make a call and move on? But here's the catch: you can't separate the person from the problem, especially if that person or problem is you. Nor is separating people from problems possible or desirable. We're irrational, emotional creatures that look to justify our decisions rationally afterwards.

You might have learned different strategies for approaching this kind of situation, like knowing your backup plan if things don't go your way. A common strategy is the 'Best Alternative to a Negotiated Agreement', or BATNA. It might seem like a good idea to have this in your back pocket when you are considering whether to walk away from a bad business deal, conversation, job or relationship. However, this is just not going to cut it when it counts because such concepts emphasise reliance on an unwinnable tug-of-war: you're trying to pull them over to your side with facts, logic and reason, but the harder you pull, the more they resist. It never worked when I was negotiating for the release of hostages, nor will it work for you when you're looking to close that important deal or manage an overwhelming situation.

Whenever you witness powerful emotions, whether in yourself or someone else, you might be inclined to try to change, improve or achieve something. This is when you might also allow fear to take over and find yourself unsure of the right thing to do. Why is it, though, that we're never satisfied with who we are right now; that we're always seeking to be further on than where we are?

Here's the thing: to develop and master your emotions and sensory acuity, it's not about desperately trying to make other stuff happen. It's about embracing what's *already* happening. In other words, it brings more curiosity than assumption to the conversation by realising it's not about you. It's about making others feel seen, heard and understood. This may be simple in theory but it's difficult to apply in practice.

Why? Because emotions make intelligent people say and do stupid things. Not only that, people don't always say what they mean. Which is why you need to get curious and find out what their underlying needs are rather than being distracted by their unhelpful words or difficult behaviour. This is not necessarily about meeting their initial demands but satisfying their human needs, such as feelings of control, belonging, safety, saving face or significance. Your words are useless until you can demonstrate enough empathy and deal with all the emotions present.

While you can't overcome emotion with logic or reason, you can work with those feelings in order to do business far more effectively. You can learn from what works in high-stakes, life-or-death emotional situations – like a kidnap-for-ransom negotiation – and use it to improve how you do business, have conversations and, ultimately, overcome challenging situations, regardless of the circumstances. In other words, don't rush to solve problems; just take your time to identify and manage emotions first.

You can do this by utilising the following Golden Ticket technique:

HARNESS YOUR RED CENTRE

People high in emotional intelligence (EQ) have the capacity to harness their Red Centre by identifying emotions they and others are experiencing. They understand how those emotions affect their thinking and use that knowledge to make better decisions.

By understanding what's going on for you (self-awareness), you can then use empathy to seek to understand what another person is feeling and ultimately make them feel seen, heard and understood.

When people feel this, they become less defensive and oppositional. They are more willing to listen to your point of view or offer. This in turn enables them to think and act from a place where they are calm, rational, balanced and grounded.

LISTEN AT LEVEL 5

Listening effectively is the cheapest and most effective way of making someone feel seen, heard and understood. What was it like the last time someone listened to you properly, giving you their complete and undivided attention? Doing this is hard work, though. Most of us think we're good at it, but the reality is much different. As Hemingway said, 'When people talk, listen completely.' It requires you to listen at 'Level 5', shifting the focus from you onto the other person. It's the most powerful Jedi mind trick of them all. Try and see for yourself.

Levels 1–3 (Focus is on YOU)

Level 1 – Listening for the GIST (Intermittent and for a minimal amount of time)

Level 2 – Listening to REBUT (Long enough until you start disagreeing with them)

Level 3 – Listening for LOGIC (Trying to pin down their internal logic for their point)

Levels 4–5 (Focus is now on the OTHER person)

Level 4 – Listening for EMOTION (What is really driving them. Use labels to clarify)

Level 5 – Listening for POINT OF VIEW (Beneath the surface for beliefs and values)

At Level 5, when people tell us what they want, we're able to hear what they're really letting us know they need. And there's a huge difference, after all, between wants and needs.

HOW TO STACK THE (EMOTIONAL) ODDS IN YOUR FAVOUR

Through rigorous adversity-proofing preparation and the effort you put into getting better at dealing with hardship, you'll be far more successful and perform better when facing it for real. Success in any field, though, is 80 per cent psychology and only 20 per cent action. For example, would you go into the street and say, 'Please push/hit/control me'? No? Yet, you probably allow others to do those things to your emotions on a daily basis, as anyone who has ever been on social media can attest to. On such platforms, you readily hand over your freedom to other people to choose how you think, feel and act. Often, when you encounter challenging situations or people you don't agree with, it's easy to become a victim of an emotional hijack and allow strong emotions to take over the thinking part of your brain.

This can make you feel frustrated, dissatisfied, inefficient and ineffective. You cannot listen properly or be persuaded to co-operate while the hijacking occurs. Not only that, but our stress levels also increase when we experience a lack of control and uncertainty about what is going to happen.

A top communicator's number one skill is managing their mindset and regulating their emotions. You can achieve this, too. But it takes time, focus and discipline. Lots of discipline. It's the same when you want to lose weight or get fitter; you don't just go to the gym once and expect immediate results. The same rules apply to the mind gym. Keep working out there, and you'll achieve your outcome of remaining objective, calm and clearheaded, regardless of what is happening.

Remember how you were taught your ABCs at school? I also learned another version when I began detective training at Scotland Yard. You can apply these to your own emotions and thoughts.

Your ABCs to emotional mastery:

Assume nothing (That your offer is so good, it's obvious the client will say 'Yes'.)

Believe no one (The hiring manager says, 'He'll fit in so well here'.)

Challenge/Check everything (Leave nothing to chance. Avoid being suspicious or cynical but always be **clarifying** and **verifying**.)

It's worth pointing out here that this is not about ignoring the rational, objective part of your brain. Far from it. We still need to think, feel and act according to our beliefs, values and principles. It's about developing the ability to distinguish between your well-tested, honed intuition and your monkey mind trying to take over. What I mean by this is that sometimes your emotions can get in the way of you performing the right action.

For example, reason tells you that exercising regularly and eating healthily is important to prevent illness and disease, and to live a healthy and enjoyable life. Yet, for most of us, at some point, there'll be times when we don't feel like exercising or eating healthily, even though we know it would be beneficial if we did. In these situations, we need to acknowledge the initial resistance and then override it with logic and reason in order to take the necessary action. When we do, that feeling of lethargy or reluctance will shift into the enjoyment and fulfilment that comes from leaning into something difficult rather than avoiding it.

EMPATHY IS A DOING WORD

Despite what you may have been told, empathy is not a concept where you absorb the other person's pain, suffering or turmoil. That's what pity is for, along with its close cousin, sympathy. These two activities are, by their very nature, selfish because you're making it all about how you feel rather than what's best for the other person. Being sympathetic with them will not help them get through their ordeal. Rather, if you can bring compassion to the situation by taking a slight step back – so you can observe but not absorb – you'll be a greater help and service to them.

How do you progress from sympathy to compassion? By walking through the doorway of empathy, which can be viewed simply as perspective-taking and demonstrating your understanding of where you think the other person is at.

To practise demonstrating empathy, follow the Empathy Loop (see the diagram below).

THE EMPATHY LOOP
How to Create Understanding

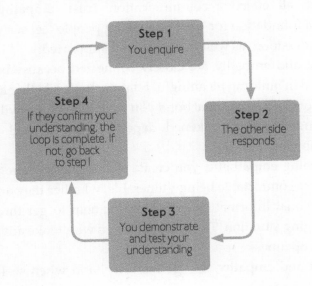

Step 1
You enquire

Step 2
The other side
responds

Step 3
You demonstrate
and test your
understanding

Step 4
If they confirm your
understanding, the
loop is complete. If
not, go back
to step 1

Ask the following questions at Step 3 with sincerity and genuine curiosity next time you're having an important conversation.

Questions to ask at Step 3:
'What I hear you saying is . . .'
'My understanding is . . . Is that right?'
'As I understand it, the problem is . . . Have I got that correct?'
'Is it OK if I share where I think you're at with this?'

Having the right mindset is also key to making this work. You can't fake genuine, empathetic listening. You may have been on the receiving end or even done it yourself – making a show of listening with head nods, the vague 'mm-mm' acknowledgements – yet you can just tell when there is no real connection.

If you empathise with someone fully, you will establish rapport and, eventually, achieve the crucial thread that runs through all effective communication: trust. Empathy helps create a foundation for trust by making people feel seen, heard and understood, as well as valued and supported.

Trust and empathy are closely connected because both are essential in building meaningful relationships, whether at home or at work. The emotional bond you have with others will either be strengthened or weakened, depending on the level of trust between you.

By being empathetic, you create a safe space where people feel more comfortable being vulnerable, whether they are sharing personal information or asking for help to get through a challenging situation. They trust that you won't take advantage of their openness.

Trust and empathy also go hand in hand when seeking to

resolve conflict or disagreement. Empathy, if done genuinely, will bridge the gap between you by showing others that you're willing to understand their perspective rather than simply trying to prove your argument at their expense. Doing so can quickly calm tensions, allowing people to trust you more, knowing you're not just thinking of your position but considering theirs too.

A relationship or business deal based on mutual trust, where both sides can demonstrate empathy, will last longer and be far more enjoyable than one based on logic and reasoning alone. This is not an either/or approach but one of and/both. In practice this could mean taking the time to empathise with a potential client and demonstrate your understanding of what the prospective deal might mean from their point of view. You set out what the future might look, sound and feel like for them. Then, you can continue to build trust by following through and doing what you say you will do. **This is how trust and credibility are achieved**. Approaching such a situation with a focus on empathy and trust, as well as logic and reasoning, will create a better environment from which to agree a business deal or partnership.

You may have been led to believe that trust can be achieved by finding common ground with whomever you're communicating with. It's not quite as straightforward as that, though. Anyone with brothers or sisters, or who has more than one child, can testify that despite having the ultimate standard of 'common ground', there are plenty of disputes, fights, yelling and sulking. Also, just because I support the same sports team as a potential client or even a kidnapper, it doesn't mean they will suddenly agree to a deal based on that fact. What we can do, though, is demonstrate our interest in and understanding of the other person's priorities and what's important to them. In other words, by 'doing empathy'.

Many people know the adage 'seek first to understand before being understood'. But this is only half the equation. If you want to take your communication ability to the next level and be able to influence and persuade anyone else, you must complete the other half. You can seek to understand all you like, but until and unless the other person believes you understand them, you won't succeed. You must get them to the place where they think, 'You get me. You are now seeing the world from my perspective.' This is irrespective of whether you agree or disagree with them.

CASE STUDY #2

Family relationships can be transformed when we demonstrate empathy, take the time to build trust and listen deeply.

When Lena, a mother of two, noticed that her teenage son, Jake, had become increasingly withdrawn and irritable, she was worried. Their once close relationship seemed to be fading, replaced by belligerence or stony silence. Her attempts to have a decent conversation with him usually ended in brief, terse exchanges. Worried about the growing distance between them, Lena realised that she needed a different approach.

Instead of allowing herself to fall into the trap of arguing with Jake, or demanding he change his behaviour, she decided to approach the situation with intention and empathy. Rather than trying to impose her own expectations, assumptions and view of the world onto the situation, she took a step back and tried hard to understand what Jake might be feeling. Remembering her own challenges as a teenager, she understood that this age is not an easy time and is usually experienced as an emotional rollercoaster.

The next day when Lena collected Jake from football practice, she gently initiated a conversation on the long drive home. Instead of bombarding him with a dozen questions, she engaged with deep Level 5 listening, making sure she didn't interrupt, as well as occasionally paraphrasing what he said.

She sought to understand what was really driving his behaviour and suspended her assumption that Jake's withdrawal and sullenness was because he didn't care about school or the family. This demonstration of empathy worked, because during the journey he opened up about the pressures he was facing at school, some friendship issues and the stress he felt with his fast-approaching exams. Lena fought the urge to immediately give advice or fix the issues.

Over time, and by being mindful of her own assumptions, consistently demonstrating empathy and listening without judgement, Lena had begun to help increase the level of trust between her and Jake, and by doing so, rebuild their relationship. As a result, Jake began to share more openly, and Lena became a source of support rather than coming across as a nagging, if well-intentioned, parent.

SUMMARY

Emotions are not obstacles to your decision-making; they are at the very heart of it.

Without them, your choices would lack depth and meaning. Far from clouding your judgement, emotions such as fear sharpen your focus, heighten your awareness and improve decision-making in challenging situations. Emotions also guide your day-to-day life, from what you eat, to what car you drive, to where you live, to who you love. They are the foundation for forming and enhancing connections with others. People with high EQ can harness their Red Centre and tune in to their feelings and those of others, and use that insight to identify and manage the emotions present, thereby creating better relationships and outcomes in many different aspects of their lives.

Listening at a deeper level (Level 5) provides a window into the other person's perspective, discovering what motivates them and their beliefs. It allows us to pick up subtle cues in tone and behaviour that reveal what a person truly needs, which is often hidden beneath the surface. This isn't just about hearing words; it's about listening to what is not being said.

To master your emotional toolkit, begin with curiosity. Don't take everything at face value. Ask questions, clarify and verify; do the facts support your intuition?

Developing your self-awareness and understanding of what's *really* going on for you enables you to empathise with others. It reduces any defensiveness they may feel and makes them more willing to listen to your point of view. This approach paves the way for more constructive dialogue and, ultimately, trust, which is like winning the emotional golden ticket.

When we understand and harness our emotions, we open the door to stronger connections and conflict resolution. It's the key to navigating the complexities of daily life and the bigger decisions. As we'll explore further, emotions and thinking are partners – two sides of the same coin – working together to shape how you live.

KEY TAKEAWAYS

1. Win the 'Emotional Golden Ticket' by tapping into your Red Centre and utilising Level 5 listening.
2. Stack the emotional odds in your favour by using your A-B-Cs.
3. Time spent empathising and building trust is seldom wasted.

PART THREE

DOING

7

Action Trumps Everything

'Mood follows action.'

Rich Roll

What we'll cover:

- **The multitasking myth**
- **Making progress or just spinning the wheels**
- **Consistency is key: routines, rituals and habits**

Everything we've covered so far, how you think and feel, has led to this point: taking meaningful action. One of the main functions of how we think and feel is to nudge us into doing something. To resolve a crisis, get through a difficult situation or make a decision. But there are also other times when your thoughts and feelings tell you that doing something is not ideal right now.

For example, you know you should go to the gym if you're trying to lose weight and become healthier, but you can't be bothered, and because you've already been a couple of times this week, surely that's enough? Plus, there's a ton of work you still need to get done, resulting in you not taking the right action.

This chapter is about how taking the right kind of action is the cure-all. Yes, you can think through problems and tune in to how you feel all day long. You can analyse, plan and prepare as much as you want. But eventually, these thoughts need to meet and engage with the outside world. Meaningful change, progress and success in life only comes from taking action, because by changing nothing, nothing changes.

Yet as we'll shortly discover, taking lots of action at the same time (i.e. multitasking) isn't the answer either. Sometimes we may also need to override our habitual thinking and emotions to do something. This is known as the action-imperative and can often be seen in newly promoted managers at work, who feel that they need to take quick actions, make big decisions, or show they are somehow 'in control' right away to justify their promotion.

Instead of them taking the time to understand the team, culture and current processes, they might rush to introduce a 'first 100 days plan', or similar, with flashy changes, like launching a new project, restructuring departments or setting ambitious (yet arbitrary) goals. They do this to show they're being proactive, but their actions may not be well planned.

Experienced employees often recognise these well-intentioned, yet flawed, moves and may feel frustrated, knowing that such rushed decisions often fail. They will do their best to keep their cynicism and eye rolling in check, having seen other leaders in the past make similar choices without fully understanding the problems or listening to the team, leading to mistakes or problems down the line. While taking decisive action is crucial in the right circumstances, if it is not well thought through it can lead to hasty decisions being made, generating unintended consequences later.

CASE STUDY #1

In 2019, a global tech company embarked on a high-stakes, time-sensitive product launch for what it saw as a revolutionary software update, intended to outpace its main competitors and capitalise on emerging AI trends. The charismatic Chief Information Security Officer (CISO) pressured colleagues and their respective teams to fast-track development. The marketing, engineering and operations teams were also working simultaneously on other major projects that couldn't be paused.

The pressure to multitask was immense. Engineers were coding while attending back-to-back meetings. The marketing department was split between promoting the new software and managing other significant campaigns. Communication gaps inevitably grew, and the workload became overwhelming. Fatigue set in as key team members worked even longer days than usual and crucial details began slipping through the cracks. Concerns and objections were raised by many but were ignored by the CISO. The chaos continued and misaligned data in product specs nearly resulted in faulty software release notes, while marketing materials were being rushed through without proper review and sign-off.

The breaking point came when the operations team realised they were about to miss an essential compliance certification – one that could have delayed the product's release by months, costing millions in lost market share. Morale was plummeting, and the team was on the brink of burnout. Recognising the impending disaster, the CEO stepped in and halted the entire project, and called for a strategic shift: a singular focus.

Having been forced to eat humble pie, the CISO restructured the workflows, assigned dedicated teams to singular tasks and eliminated as many distractions as possible. The new mantra became that of 'the one thing', i.e. concentrating on just the one thing that matters most in that moment. The engineering team concentrated solely on the final code, ensuring all features were fully functional. The marketing team refocused their energy on building the campaign around the new product launch, without additional projects competing for attention. Clear, focused communication became the priority.

Several weeks later the teams completed their tasks with precision, and the product launched without a hitch. The company not only met its deadlines but also received rave reviews and learned a valuable lesson in prioritising deep work over multitasking. This shift in approach saved the company from a costly mistake and improved the team's morale and long-term productivity.

THE MULTITASKING MYTH

Focus has become our most scarce resource. For most of us, it can often feel like we're being bombarded with stimulation, information and requests from the moment we wake up until we fall asleep at night. Our inability to focus on what matters and prioritise effectively can lead us to take the wrong type of action. This results in overwhelm, burnout and increased stress levels, particularly when we are facing adversity. We often think we're being productive by juggling all the urgent demands competing for our attention, time and energy. But there is a single, clear productivity killer. Here's a hint: it's not your smartphone!

It's multitasking. This type of action is one of our most drain-ing and debilitating behaviours. Despite what you may believe, multitasking does not exist. What you're actually doing is rapidly shifting your attention back and forth between things. It is exhausting and energy-intensive for your brain and body, and it can negatively impact your ability to think, feel and act effectively, particularly in the moments that count. But you've probably already found that out for yourself from your own experience.

The global leadership development consultancy, Potential Project has studied multitasking extensively. They argue that this energy-draining task-switching behaviour is caused by the 'PAID reality' most of us find ourselves in, which is wrecking the quality of our lives:

Pressured
Always-on
Information overload
Distracted

While multitasking may seem like an effective way to handle multiple tasks simultaneously, there are ten significant negative consequences of doing so.

1. **Reduced quality of work**: When you're juggling multiple tasks, the quality of your work on each task may suffer. Dividing your attention can lead to errors, oversights and incomplete work.

2. **Decreased productivity**: Contrary to common belief, multitasking can decrease overall productivity. The brain must switch between tasks, and this context-switching incurs a cognitive cost, leading to a slower completion of tasks.

3. **Increased stress**: Managing multiple tasks at once can be stressful, as it puts additional mental pressure on you.

Stress levels may rise, leading to a negative impact on your overall well-being.

4. **Impaired memory**: Multitasking can negatively affect memory consolidation. Information processed during multi-tasking may not be stored as effectively in long-term memory, leading to difficulties in recalling details later.

5. **Decreased creativity**: Creativity often requires focused attention. Multitasking may hinder your ability to think deeply and creatively about a particular problem or task.

6. **Inefficient time management**: Constantly switching between tasks can make it difficult to manage your time effectively. It's challenging to estimate accurately how much time each task requires when multitasking.

7. **Increased likelihood of mistakes**: Multitasking increases the likelihood of making mistakes, as your attention is divided, and you may overlook important details or steps in a task.

8. **Impact on relationships**: Multitasking can also affect personal relationships. When you're not fully present in a conversation or activity, it may lead to misunderstandings and communication breakdowns.

9. **Fatigue and burnout**: Constantly multitasking can be mentally exhausting. Over time, it may contribute to fatigue and burnout, affecting your performance and well-being.

10. **Difficulty in task switching**: The human brain isn't designed to switch seamlessly between tasks. It takes time to refocus and readjust to a new task, leading to inefficiencies in task-switching.

Multitasking is destroying your progress, whether you're attempting it at home or at work. It's understandable you might think you have too much to do and insufficient time to do it all. Your to-do list is never completed, and items always get carried over to the next day. Sound familiar?

All is not lost, though. You can overcome this multitasking trap and rewire your brain to develop a clearer sense of what you should be prioritising, increase your focus and follow through, no matter how challenging the circumstances. There are many proven alternatives to multitasking, all of which help you improve your focus, productivity and efficiency. Find the one that consistently works well for you.

One technique that I used to write this book, while having a heavy travel schedule, as well as delivering keynote talks and workshops, not to mention family responsibilities, was the Pomodoro Technique. It's a simple time-management method that helps you stay focused and get more done. It's a great way of staying focused by breaking work into small, manageable chunks, with short breaks in between.

Why is this, and other similar techniques, so effective? They work on the principle of focused intervals, to avoid cognitive overload and maintain our attention span. For some in-depth tasks, a longer interval of 45–90 minutes might be required, which still works on the same basis. Most of us know the feeling of procrastinating for ages to get something done, but as the deadline approaches it somehow enhances our focus and productivity by creating a sense of urgency. This aligns with Parkinson's Law, which states, 'work expands to fill the time available for its completion'. Having regular time-defined periods set aside for work can also help with habit formation and building a sustainable and effective routine.

Here's how it works:

1. Choose a task.
2. Set a timer for 25 minutes (25 minutes = 1 Pomodoro).
3. Work on the task until the timer rings.
4. Take a 5-minute break.
5. Repeat as required.
6. After four Pomodoros, take a longer break of 15 to 30 minutes.

I use Focus To-Do (a free Google Chrome extension https://www.focustodo.cn) for the timer.

Besides the Pomodoro Technique, you can try several other techniques and strategies to enhance your concentration. Some are quick and easy, such as disabling pop-ups and turning off notifications on your phone or laptop, prioritising only direct messages from significant individuals or groups, e.g. key leadership or team members, or using airplane mode or the do not disturb function on your phone. Would you rather multitask for six unfocused hours or work four laser-focused hours and complete ALL your important tasks? The choice is yours.

Here are some alternative strategies to enhance your concentration:

52–17 Method: This technique is like the Pomodoro Technique but with longer work intervals. You work for 52 minutes and then take a 17-minute break. This cycle is based on research suggesting that the most productive people work for around 52 minutes before needing a break.

90-minute work blocks: Divide your workday into 90-minute blocks of focused work, followed by a longer break. This aligns with the natural ultradian rhythm of the body, allowing you to maintain high energy and concentration.

Batching: Group similar tasks together and tackle them during specific time blocks. This reduces the cognitive load of switching between different types of work, allowing you to maintain focus on similar tasks for an extended period.

Time blocking: Allocate specific blocks of time for different types of tasks such as emails. This helps you create a routine and sets clear boundaries for each activity, preventing distractions and promoting focus during designated time periods.

The two-minute rule: If a task takes less than two minutes to complete, do it immediately. This prevents small tasks from accumulating and disrupting your focus on more significant tasks.

Deep work sessions: Allocate extended periods of time (e.g. 2–4 hours) for deep, undisturbed work. During these sessions, eliminate all possible distractions and focus solely on the task at hand.

Mindfulness and meditation: Practise mindfulness or meditation to train your mind to stay present and focused. Even short sessions of 5–10 minutes can help improve your ability to concentrate.

The Eisenhower Matrix: Focus on tasks that are both urgent and important first, then move down the list. Ignore tasks that you categorise as not urgent and not important. Life's too short!

Multitasking while communicating

Whenever I was negotiating for the release of hostages or access to the decryption keys to resolve a ransomware attack, the temptation to multitask was immense. There were lots of things that needed to be done quickly and not enough people to do them. Yet multitasking during high-stakes negotiations, whether in your business or personal life, poses significant dangers and risks, potentially undermining the success of the negotiation itself.

Further to the consequences we highlighted earlier, here are some additional specific dangers associated with multitasking when the stakes are high:

1. **Impaired decision-making** by reducing the quality and depth of analysis and assessment, potentially leading to suboptimal choices.
2. **Communication breakdown** results in you missing important verbal and non-verbal cues from the other party, leading to misunderstandings or misinterpretations.
3. **Loss of focus on priorities**, resulting in you being unable to keep track of key issues and maintaining a strategic approach because your attention is divided.
4. **Reduced empathy and rapport** can diminish your ability to connect emotionally, potentially harming the relationship.
5. **Missed opportunities** could impact the overall success of the negotiation and the potential for achieving a mutually beneficial agreement. Can also compromise or overlook creative solutions.
6. **Escalation of tension** and hindering the ability to reach some form of resolution, cooperation or collaboration.

7. **Lack of strategic thinking** thereby making it difficult to navigate complex issues and make informed decisions.
8. **Negative perception** towards you by your counterpart, who might view your multitasking as a lack of respect or commitment to the negotiation process. This can harm the overall atmosphere and trust between you.

To mitigate these dangers, prioritising focus and concentration during important conversations is crucial. Effective decision-making often requires mindfulness, active listening towards others and a comprehensive understanding of the issues, none of which can be achieved while multitasking.

Multitasking might seem productive initially, but if you do everything at once, you do nothing at all. It's getting in the way of you achieving your goals by increasing switching costs, causing mistakes, draining creativity and impairing memory.

Try some of the above techniques to build the habit of focus and you'll unlock true and satisfying productivity. Managing your focus and attention immeasurably improves the quality of your life.

MAKING PROGRESS OR JUST SPINNING THE WHEELS

Having advised and coached thousands of leaders and business owners over the years, I am aware they all lament a lack of time to do everything that they wanted to. For them, every waking moment is filled with competing demands, from scrambling for cost-reduction measures to firefighting a never-ending stream of incidents, before doing their best to deal with the main strategic issues.

When I was deployed during a kidnapping, extortion or similar crisis, I acted as a trusted advisor to the senior decision-makers, whether they were a country director or one of the C-suite executives. I wasn't there to make decisions for them, but to advise on the pros and cons of viable options and give my recommendations. Regardless of location, industry or sector, I noticed that these highly professional, yet very busy, leaders all displayed similar traits and habits. They would rush from meeting to meeting, check their email constantly and make countless phone calls, dousing flames as they went. In other words, there was a huge amount of fast-moving activity that allowed no time for reflection, analysis and consideration. But these are all activities that are crucial for creating new ideas, determining how best to manage and mitigate risk, and, crucially, where they need to place their most valuable resource – their focus.

Most leaders have far too much to do despite regularly working long hours. Yet the fact is, very few of them use their time as effectively as possible. They often think they're attending to pressing matters, but they're just spinning their wheels. When you are facing a high-risk, high-pressure situation, this can prove catastrophic.

The *Harvard Business Review* article, 'Beware the Busy Manager', describes unproductive busyness as 'active non-action'. The authors also discovered, from their decade-long, in-depth study of a dozen global organisations, that a staggering 90 per cent of managers squandered their time on ineffective activities. But what was the difference between the 90 per cent who did and the 10 per cent who didn't?

The authors of the article found that the managers who took effective action demonstrated two traits: focus and energy. Think of **focus** as concentrated attention – the ability to zero in on a goal and see the task through to completion. Focused managers aren't in reactive mode; they choose not to respond immediately to every issue that comes their way or get sidetracked from their goals by distractions like email, meetings, setbacks and unforeseen demands. Because they clearly understand what they want to accomplish, they carefully weigh their options before selecting a course of action.

The article goes on to describe how the second characteristic, **energy**, is the vigour fuelled by intense personal commitment. This energy allows managers to be pulled along rather than constantly pushing (which is more tiring), and to go the extra mile when tackling heavy workloads and meeting tight deadlines.

For example, the team that created the Sony Vaio computer – the first PC to let users combine other Sony technologies, such as digital cameras, portable music players and camcorders – showed a lot of energy. Responding to CEO Nobuyuki Idei's challenge to create an integrated technological playground for a burgeoning generation of 'digital dream kids', Hiroshi Nakagawa and his team put in 100-hour weeks to create the kind of breakthrough product Idei hoped for. One manager, Kazumasa Sato, was so devoted to the project that he spent three years conducting consumer reconnaissance in electronics shops every weekend. Sato's research into consumer buying patterns helped Sony develop a shop layout that enhanced traffic flow and, by extension, sales. Ultimately, the Vaio captured a significant share of the Japanese PC market.

This example is not an advert for everyone to suddenly start working 100-hour weeks, but to highlight that your intention matters, and when it aligns with your purpose in life, you'll be pleasantly surprised how putting in occasionally long hours can, counter-intuitively, give you more drive and energy rather than less.

While focus and energy are positive traits, neither alone is sufficient to produce the kind of purposeful action organisations need most from their managers. Focus without energy devolves into listless execution or leads to burnout. Without focus, energy dissipates into purposeless busyness or, in its most destructive form, a series of wasteful failures.

The Focus-Energy Matrix below identifies four types of behaviour that highlight the characteristics of purposeful and non-productive activities: Disengagement, Procrastination, Distraction and Purposefulness.

The Focus-Energy Matrix

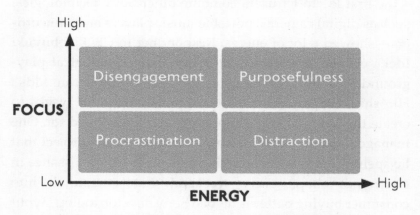

Courtesy of Heike Bruch and Sumantra Ghoshal

Some organisations breed a firefighting culture, where the energy is often high without any opportunity to recharge and refocus. Such workplace environments often result in poor employee engagement, high staff turnover and low productivity.

On a kidnapping case, I would often spend the first few days working with the senior leaders of the crisis management team to build a flexible 'battle rhythm'. In other words, a natural ebb and flow of sustainable activity fuelled by a powerful purposefulness – the safe and timely release of the hostages – while also ensuring time was deliberately spent every day on relaxing and recovery activities. Also, I made sure they cleared their schedules of non-important work, which they were able to delegate to others.

We would always seek to focus on the underlying interests and needs of the hostage-takers rather than just their position or demand. This can be applied to everyday life. Focusing on the core concerns of whomever you're communicating with will enable you to minimise distraction or disengagement, eventually find mutually acceptable solutions and achieve a positive outcome.

'Motivation is what gets you started. Habit is what keeps you going.'

Jim Ryun

CONSISTENCY IS KEY: ROUTINES, RITUALS AND HABITS

Our routines, rituals and habits are like the secret sauce of success. They are the small actions we repeat consistently until they become automatic and ingrained in our daily lives. Successful people who can thrive regardless of circumstances prioritise their routines, rituals and habits. It's not that they have more time in the day; they use it more wisely by building empowering habits.

These can be positive or negative, shaping our lives more than we realise. Setting and maintaining an effective routine has many benefits. There are no hard and fast rules, and the efficacy of routines, rituals and habits is that they are specific to the individual.

For people with high-stress jobs, starting the day with, for example, exercise or some form of mindfulness practice can get them off to a positive and productive start. Others may prefer to focus on an evening routine that allows them to consolidate and reflect on the day, while setting themselves up for a good night's sleep.

That said, there are some fundamentals to increasing overall health and well-being and making more effective decisions throughout your day. Regularly checking your mobile phone immediately upon waking up and while still in bed will potentially set a reactive tone for your day. Whereas if you get up and, rather than pick up your phone, go for a walk, go to the gym or read, it's likely to give you more clarity, focus and energy.

By way of an example, I do the following three micro-habits as part of my evening routine every night:

PLAN THE NEXT DAY (10 minutes)

Why? Writing down a list of everything I need to get done gets it out of my head. It stops it from swirling around my brain while I try to fall asleep. From this (often long) list, I then highlight the top three priorities for the following day. There are usually more than three but selecting only the top three helps me to focus on what's really important (rather than just urgent).

Again, writing this down somehow relaxes my brain, knowing that I won't forget them and that there's a plan to deal with it tomorrow – so for now, I can relax. At this point, I make sure my phone is in airplane mode or on do not disturb, and I don't need to pick it up again until at least an hour after waking up the following morning.

HOT BATH/SHOWER (20 minutes)

Why? It helps me fall asleep more quickly (within 10 minutes of getting into bed without fail), and I have better-quality sleep throughout the night. It does this because, counter-intuitively, it promotes heat loss from my core, which is a significant factor in the onset of deep sleep. Plus, there's the good old-fashioned reason that I find it relaxing. I also use that time to process stuff from the day. Many of the conversations I need to have, talks I need to deliver, or chapters I need to write have started in my head while relaxing in the bath or shower. It means, however, that when I get out, I have to write it all down quickly – but this does get it out of my head and onto the page – thereby once again freeing up valuable space in my brain before I get into bed.

GRATITUDE (5 minutes)

Why? No matter how stressful or overwhelming the day has been, no matter how many things didn't go according to plan, I spend a few minutes thinking of things, people or situations I can be grateful for. Not in an intellectual, tick-box way, hurrying through it so it's just another thing to get done, but in a genuine, feel-it-in-my-body kind of way. Once I feel grateful and appreciative, it dilutes any negative emotions or thoughts that I may have been experiencing. If my kids or partner are there, I also make sure we have proper, heart-felt hugs so they know they are deeply loved and cared for, despite whatever day they've had or challenges they may be going through. Plus, I get a serotonin boost from this. Then, when my head rests on the pillow, I can let go of the day and relax into a restful sleep.

I do these micro-habits because, like most people, my days usually involve being bombarded with stimulation, information, requests and noise from when I wake up until it's time for bed. If I'm not kept in check by these habits, I can end up feeling overwhelmed, burned out and stressed. None of which are conducive to living a good life.

And by way of caveat, I'm far from perfect in applying these steps every night. If I do them for 80 per cent of my evenings, I don't self-flagellate over missing the remaining 20 per cent because I might be out for dinner, travelling or otherwise in the middle of enjoying myself.

In recent years, many authors, such as James Clear, Charles Duhigg and B. J. Fogg, have written all about the importance of habits. They've each highlighted how cultivating successful ones can enable you to succeed despite living a busy life.

A summary of the key fundamentals of habit formation:

The power of marginal gains. Start small while thinking big and implement tiny improvements over time – it will yield remarkable results. Focusing on small, actionable changes can gradually transform your habits and, consequently, your life.

The four laws of behaviour change: cue, craving, response and reward. Firstly, a **cue** triggers your brain to start a behaviour. This leads to a **craving**, the desire or motivation to act. Then comes the **response**, the actual habit or action you take. Finally, the **reward** is a positive feeling or result you get from doing the behaviour, reinforcing it and making you more likely to repeat it. Together, these steps create a loop that builds lasting habits.

Identity-based habits. You can cultivate lasting change by aligning the desired behaviour with the person you aspire to become. Shifting your focus from outcomes to identity and values fosters a deeper commitment to your habits and enhances your resilience in adversity.

Celebrating small wins. Doing so can serve as a catalyst for habit formation. By acknowledging and rewarding incremental progress, you can cultivate a positive feedback loop, reinforcing the desired behaviours and bolstering resilience in the face of setbacks.

Anchoring habits to existing routines. Anchoring new habits to existing routines, such as performing squats while waiting for the kettle to boil, can act as a strategy for habit integration and sustainability. By piggybacking new behaviours onto established patterns, it becomes easier to incorporate them into your daily life.

Incorporating these insights into your daily practices empowers you to cultivate successful routines, rituals and habits that propel you towards your aspirations and equip you with the resilience to thrive in adversity.

There are many well-respected experts who all share similar perspectives on the importance of a holistic approach to mental and physical health. Andrew Huberman, Professor of Neurobiology and Ophthalmology at Stanford School of Medicine, is one of them, and he provides eight scientifically proven mental and physical health pillars. They can help you deal with adversity with relative ease if they are applied regularly, and they will put you in the best possible frame of mind to make better decisions as you go about your day.

The eight pillars are:

1. **Sleep**: Consistent, high-quality sleep is essential for brain function, mood regulation and overall physical health.

2. **Light (Sun): (particularly first and last thing in the day)**: Exposure to natural light outdoors in the morning and evening helps regulate your circadian rhythms, improving sleep and alertness.

3. **Exercise**: Regular physical activity supports brain and body health, enhances mood and helps manage stress.

4. **Stress management**: Effectively managing stress through techniques like mindfulness, breathing exercises or physical activity helps protect mental and physical health.

5. **Relationships (including to self)**: Positive relationships with others and maintaining a healthy connection with oneself are crucial for emotional well-being and stress reduction.

6. **Nutrients**: A nutrient-rich diet supports brain and body function, influencing energy levels, mood and long-term health.

7. **Oral health and gut microbiome**: Oral health and a balanced gut microbiome play critical roles in overall health, affecting digestion, immunity and even mental health.

8. **Spiritual grounding**: Finding purpose, meaning or a sense of connection, whether through spirituality, meditation or other practices, enhances emotional and mental resilience.

CASE STUDY #2

Mike, a forty-year-old father of two, found himself constantly drained and frustrated with his health. Between long hours at work, family responsibilities and the stress of everyday life, he barely had time to take care of himself. His exercise routine was inconsistent – non-existent if he was really being honest – meals were often rushed or unhealthy, and his sleep was sporadic at best.

One evening, at the end of a particularly exhausting week, Mike collapsed on the sofa in front of the TV as usual. As he sat there, not really focusing, he knew he was tired of feeling tired and it was time for a change. But although he wanted to feel better, the idea of overhauling his lifestyle seemed overwhelming and just too much. Out of the corner of his eye, he caught sight of a book about how someone had turned their life around by being consistent in doing healthy habits. His wife had bought it for him for his last birthday, almost a year ago. It had remained untouched since.

Fascinated by how they had overcome challenge after challenge despite the best efforts of life and the doubt of those closest to them, Mike was gripped and ended up reading the book from cover to cover that evening. Instead of aiming for an intense workout programme or a strict diet that would not be sustainable in the long run, he started small. He created a morning routine he could stick to; waking up thirty minutes earlier than usual to take a brisk walk around the neighbourhood and drink a tall glass of water before getting on with his day. It was so simple – it almost felt too simple at first – but as the days turned into weeks, Mike began to notice a difference.

Gradually, that short walk became a twenty-minute jog. As his energy levels increased, he found himself naturally choosing healthier options for lunch and cutting back on fast food. He didn't overhaul his diet overnight, but small shifts – like packing protein-rich snacks and choosing wholefoods – began to stick.

Mike also committed to winding down earlier in the evenings, improving his sleep by limiting late-night screen time and setting a consistent bedtime. These simple habits became part of his daily routine, helping him sleep better and feel more refreshed each morning.

By stacking several simple habits, within six months Mike had not only shed extra weight but also drastically reduced his stress and felt physically stronger. What made the biggest difference wasn't some extreme fitness programme or unsustainable diet. It was the small, consistent changes – regular movement, better hydration and nutrition, and improved sleep – that Mike built into his routine. His journey shows that real, lasting improvements in health come from steady, manageable habits that anyone can incorporate into their busy lives.

SUMMARY

In this chapter, we explored the critical role of taking action in achieving meaningful change. While thoughts and emotions are essential for decision-making, they must lead to action for progress to occur. Too often, you are likely to let emotions or distractions prevent you from taking the steps you need to move forward, whether it's skipping the gym or delaying making an important decision. Ultimately, change only happens when you engage with the outside world and take consistent action.

One key insight is the myth of multitasking, a major productivity killer. Despite its allure, multitasking is inefficient, draining and often results in poor work quality, increased stress and even impaired memory. We learned how the modern-day workplace and home fuels this habit: at times you may feel pressured, always-on, overwhelmed by information and distracted. Yet research shows that single-tasking is far more effective, allowing you to conserve energy, reduce mistakes and be more creative.

We also looked at several practical ways for you to overcome multitasking, such as the Pomodoro Technique and time-blocking strategies that prioritise focused, deliberate work. Research tells us that such methods help improve concentration and efficiency, freeing you from the constant task-switching that can drain your mental energy.

Ultimately, while you may feel overwhelmed by multiple demands placed upon your time and attention, true productivity and success come from mastering focus and taking consistent, meaningful action. Developing habits that prioritise single-tasking and focus leads to improved decision-making, creativity and resilience in the face of challenges.

KEY TAKEAWAYS

1. Stay focused on one task at a time.
2. Avoid busyness for the sake of being busy.
3. Small steps consistently applied equals sustained success.

8

Crises and Conflicts

'Comfort and growth can never coexist.'
Ginni Rometty, former chairman,
president and CEO of IBM

What we'll cover:

- **Conflict and crisis resolution**
- **Flex your decision-making muscles**
- **Dealing with difficult people**

So far, you've learned how to develop sensory acuity to tune in to and regulate your emotions effectively, as well as being able to expand your precious focus and awareness, before choosing what and how you'll think and the subsequent action you'll take. By taking these steps consciously, you're gradually increasing your ability to embrace uncertainty and take adversity in your stride. Why is this important? Because remember, the quality of your life is directly proportional to your ability to withstand and navigate uncertainty.

As I hope you realise now, if you think you're going to sail through life with everything and everyone fitting in with your view of how the world should be, you're in for a shock. The reality is that your best-laid plans will only get you so far and probably won't survive 'first contact with the enemy'. What (or who) is this enemy? For most of us, it will present itself in the form of crises and conflicts. These will look, sound and feel different for each of us. For some, a relatively minor episode, such as not getting the job we wanted or being cut up by an inconsiderate driver, is enough to qualify. For others, it will take something far more dramatic.

Regardless of where you'd place yourself on that spectrum, crises and conflicts are a fact of life, which is why they shouldn't be feared, and, in fact, should be embraced at every available opportunity. This chapter will explore how you can do that.

CASE STUDY #1

Early one morning, while you're busy making breakfast, your mobile phone rings. It takes you by surprise as you glance at the clock on the wall and see that it's not even 7 a.m. yet. Answering the call, you recognise the voice. It's Steve, a work colleague of your spouse. You've only spoken to him a couple of times previously, mainly at work social functions as a guest of your partner. You sense hesitancy in his voice. In that split second, uncertainty begins to churn in your stomach.

'I have some terrible news . . .' is all you hear. Your knees buckle and your hand grabs the edge of the table to stop you from crashing to the floor. You take a few deep breaths and eventually manage to compose yourself.

Steve slowly explains how they suspect your loved one was abducted a few hours earlier with three other colleagues while travelling overseas. Witnesses have described how all four of them were bundled into the back of a white van at gunpoint. Instinctively, you key your partner's number into your phone, but the call doesn't connect.

Your throat tightens as rising panic threatens to choke you.

No one has heard from them or the kidnappers since. No ransom demand has been made.

Steve explains that the company has a special risks insurance policy specifically for situations like this. You should expect a call from a crisis response consultant who will advise you on what to do next, particularly if the kidnappers call. You slump into a chair and know at that very moment your life will never be the same again.

This situation may seem far-fetched, yet a version of it is played out worldwide daily. Until a demand has been received, kidnap-for-ransom negotiations usually start out as a missing person enquiry because it's not known for sure exactly what has happened. Witnesses to any crime are human and, therefore, sometimes fallible. However, in this scenario, it can safely be assumed that the witnesses are reliable, and the location and manner of the abduction is consistent with previous kidnappings.

Thousands of miles away, I receive a phone call from one of my colleagues telling me what had happened. Having obtained the scant details, I place two calls: one to you as the family member and the other to the company of your loved one. Time is of the essence; the actions taken in the first 24–48 hours impact the chances of getting your spouse back safely and in a timely manner.

Anyone who has ever served in the military or law enforcement will be familiar with the concept of 'hurry up and wait'. This strategy involves lots of initial activity, energy and decision-making, only for it all to give way quickly to anticipatory stillness and calm. One might be forgiven for feeling frustrated as the initial burst of energy dissipates into what could be seen as simply hanging around waiting for something, anything, to happen.

Nothing could be further from the truth. Moving quickly, making key decisions and taking focused, determined action enables us to set up and be prepared for when the real challenge begins. I advise you and the company to take the following immediate steps while I jump on a plane and make my way to sit alongside you and do whatever it takes to get your loved one back.

CONFLICT AND CRISIS RESOLUTION

Being able to embrace and resolve conflict and crises can dramatically improve the quality of your life. In this section we're going to explore some of the proven ways you can do so, no matter what you're facing.

The first step is to realise that life is not a solo sport. We're social creatures that thrive when we are engaging with and supporting others. Yes, you might be able to be ruthless and succeed by yourself a few times. But if you want that success repeatedly, you can go much further, and for longer, together. In the kidnapping scenario above, my first advice to the family is to identify and form a **Crisis Management Team (CMT)**.

This consists of the smallest, odd number of people possible (ideally 3–5 maximum to avoid a stalemate when it comes to voting on a decision), who will be responsible for agreeing on the negotiation strategy and making all the key decisions to get the hostage released. As the crisis response consultant, one of my main roles is to advise this group, providing them with options and recommendations. While you're unlikely to have to establish a CMT to negotiate the release of a loved one, still consider who will be in your version of a CMT to help advise and support you to get through and overcome whatever challenge you're facing. Having such a team prevents people from going 'off-script' by taking the wrong action that could potentially jeopardise your success. Often, we don't even need advice. Sometimes, a safe, confidential sounding board is all that is required. This might be other trusted family members, friends or colleagues whose counsel you value.

The next step is to **obtain a 'clean phone'** to communicate with the kidnappers. When they first contact the hostage's family or company, we give them this number. We also inform anyone who might receive a call from the kidnappers that they should direct them to this number if they make contact. This is important, as in the initial stages of an abduction, kidnappers will look to sow confusion and open multiple negotiations to extract as much money as possible. This can be prevented by shutting down all these other options and only having one contact number.

In our everyday lives, we often witness people playing one person off against another, sowing seeds of dissent, discord and disarray. Occasionally, we find ourselves being the victim of this. In the workplace, this might involve a colleague spreading malicious and unfounded gossip about us, having taken a situation out of context to diminish your credibility in the eyes of your boss. The 'clean phone' concept is about controlling what is being said and how it is being communicated.

Schedule regular catch-ups with your team or boss to ensure that too much time doesn't go by where others can control the narrative about you.

Once you have your 'clean phone', you next need to **identify an individual** who can act as the '**communicator**' between the CMT and the kidnappers. They must be a psychologically and emotionally resilient individual who can easily withstand personal insults and threats, as the kidnappers will test them. My role here is to train, coach and support the communicator in what to say, as well as how and when to say it. The alternative is confusion and chaos, with multiple parties all playing one another off against each other. Building on the 'clean phone' concept above, consider whether you are the best person to have that all-too-pressing difficult conversation. Do you need to suspend your ego and allow a trusted colleague or friend to have it instead?

Finally, it's important to **know your desired outcome** of that initial call with the kidnappers. While the specifics may vary slightly from case to case, several principles still apply. These include reassuring them that you are taking them seriously, obtaining proof that your loved one is alive and that the kidnappers must continue to look after them and treat them well if they want to be paid something. Above all, make no promises and don't lie. If you do, it'll come back to bite you. Hard.

This approach can be applied to all areas of your life. Unless you know what you want from any given situation, how do you know in which direction to head? Otherwise, if you don't, you're likely to find yourself drifting aimlessly like a boat out at sea without a sail or engine.

Just as a kidnapping will take you by surprise and automatically activate your hard-wired evolutionary response to either stay and fight, run away or freeze, so will more everyday surges of adversity. Taking quick, bold action in those first few hours eventually provides you with the necessary breathing space to pause, reflect and respond consciously and deliberately to the various challenges and problems that will inevitably arise later. This initial burst of activity enables you to get to the start line in great shape, confident that no matter what happens, you can take it all in your stride and overcome it.

The applicability and benefits of this concept are played out in many areas of our lives. For example, the 'abduction' metaphor can be any situation in which you're taken by complete and utter surprise, and which has potentially high stakes. This could be the unexpected withdrawal of a lucrative business deal that you thought was a dead cert, or when the purchase of your dream home suddenly falls through. Regardless of the context, it requires you to take immediate action to get an initial grip so you can then consider, decide and respond far more effectively.

Having one decision-making authority (CMT) with a clear, focused outcome, using one number with one resilient and emotionally regulated voice, which communicates one message, increases your chances of resolving any challenging situation, whether that is the release and recovery of a hostage or overcoming the crisis that you and your family or organisation are facing.

How to resolve conflict

As a kidnap-for-ransom negotiator, I learned six crisis-resolution skills that apply equally well to all areas of our lives, not just when in the unusual situation of trying to release hostages.

Skill #1: Listening

The NYPD hostage negotiation team's motto is 'Talk to me'. This nicely demonstrates that you are ready to listen (as opposed to talking). Active listening is more a mindset than a checklist of 'to-dos', and is a key first step in building trust and rapport and demonstrating empathy. Listening deeply develops a sense of being heard.

Skill #2: Patience

Slow down and don't rush to solve problems. By being patient, you avoid the trap of jumping to conclusions. Taking your time also dissipates high emotion and can help build rapport.

Skill #3: Respect

If you're judging or dismissing the person with whom you're trying to resolve a conflict, it will prevent respect from being felt. And until the other person feels this, they are unlikely to change their behaviour according to your wishes.

Skill #4: Calmness

Portraying a sense of calm while the storm rages around you is one of the most crucial conflict resolution skills and is relevant for all communication in general.

Skill #5: Self-awareness

Developing high levels of sensory acuity and emotional intelligence (EQ) enables you to display self-awareness. This helps you communicate more effectively without losing sight of your ultimate outcome or being forced into an agreement you don't want.

Skill #6: Adaptability

Rarely does a tense conversation or crisis resolve itself, or as initially planned. Being agile and flexible to the changing circumstances will help you achieve your goals.

Resolving crises and conflicts in your organisation

While you're unlikely to face the emotional complexity of a kidnap negotiation, the everyday conversations you have and decisions you need to make, particularly when faced with a crisis, still rely upon trust, rapport and a mutual sense of respect. Likewise, when you are dealing with difficult people in your daily life, active listening and a respectful, calm demeanour are proven techniques for preserving your relationship.

In addition to the six skills listed above, I learned a further set of strategies that can also help you resolve crises and conflicts and make tough decisions.

1. **Preparation.** Before negotiations began in earnest with the kidnappers, I would always sit down and discuss our negotiation strategy with the family or company CMT (i.e. what we would say to the kidnappers and why), and our financial strategy (how much we should pay them and why). We would also discuss how we would overcome all the threats, obstacles, issues and challenges likely to be presented. In a wider business context, you might consider agreeing with a new supplier on how to deal with disputes should they arise.

2. **Boundaries.** I've found establishing boundaries at the outset helpful to avoid issues escalating into a full-blown crisis. This might be as simple as agreeing to be honest, never making promises you can't fulfil and treating all parties with respect. Doing so at the beginning makes it much more likely you and they will abide by these considerations when tensions are running high. It gives you the space to deliver a 'positive no',

because you've taken the time and energy to establish that golden thread in all successful conversations: trust.

3. **Identify emotions early.** In every hostage-taking, kidnapping or other similar negotiation or conversation I've been involved in, intense emotions threatened to run the show. Thankfully, there are some effective strategies for managing and diffusing them. These can be as simple as being present with, and listening deeply to, the other person. Active listening techniques like emotional labelling involves identifying and reflecting on the emotions you believe the other person is experiencing. As you now know, we call this 'name it to tame it'. It's highly effective and makes the other person feel heard. In all negotiation contexts, time spent exploring the other person's emotions is seldom wasted.

4. **Buy time.** It is natural and understandable to want to resolve a crisis or tense conversation quickly. However, it can prove beneficial to slow the process down and buy yourself time. This usually ends in a better deal. Why? Because it allows powerful emotions to subside and more rational, objective thinking to occur. Imagine being paid by the hour rather than a set fee. This will give you the incentive to take your time to work through challenges methodically and come up with the best deal possible. This works effectively when the other side demands a swift resolution and agreement.

5. **Cooperation and collaboration.** Your desired outcome in all types of high-stakes communication, from the home to the workplace, should be that of finding a way to cooperate or collaborate with the other person as

much as you can. You'll never build a long-lasting relationship with them otherwise, not to mention the risk of you losing out on future lucrative deals.

Resolving virtual conflicts

When you are resolving a conflict, it's better to talk face to face instead of emailing. Using any form of electronic communication often causes more problems than it solves. Trying to connect through email is challenging. There are no nonverbal cues to pick up on and people might be unsure about the social rules, causing you to be inadvertently rude or less considerate.

Communicating over email can also lead to many misunderstandings as it's tricky to convey emotions and tone accurately. It can also exacerbate any conflict that arises and result in a game of email tennis, where each side reacts emotionally, firing off emails back and forth. If the issue is still unresolved after two emails, don't let it go to a third round of volleys. Take it offline and pick up the phone or sit face to face to work through it.

You'll find below four ways to resolve conflict, whether at work or at home, that are particularly effective when you need to have a difficult conversation or provide feedback. Often, the greatest challenges we need to face are actually on our own side. Dealing with the client, customer, neighbour or kidnapper is relatively easy in comparison. It is our colleagues, boss or family that often trigger us, that provide the most resistance or appear to effortlessly drain our enthusiasm. We refer to this as the 'crisis within the crisis', and in a kidnapping case it would take up about 80 per cent of my time. By adopting these strategies, you can develop the courage to navigate challenges, including those everyday confrontations, and give and receive more effective feedback.

1. **Be comfortable with being uncomfortable:** Initiate difficult conversations regularly to strengthen your courage muscle. Over time, facing discomfort becomes more manageable.

2. **Tackle necessary changes quickly:** Avoiding necessary changes only prolongs issues. Confront challenges directly. Say what needs to be said. Do what needs to be done.

3. **Listen to your intuition:** Pay attention to your inner knowing. If something doesn't feel right, it's a sign to act. Ignored problems often escalate.

4. **Endure challenges:** Leading through change demands enduring discomfort. It requires courage and patience to overcome resistance.

FLEX YOUR DECISION-MAKING MUSCLES

Humans are the only creatures that can choose what meaning we assign to our experiences. We can often find the positive in a situation and even change our story in a deep and meaningful way. We don't always have to let our circumstances define us. Those with inner strength can decide to face tough decisions head-on and use them to become stronger. They take responsibility for themselves because they realise they are the architect of their lives and make decisions accordingly.

Obstacles that can get in your way include:

Cognitive biases and heuristics

A heuristic is a mental shortcut that guides your decision-making and helps you make choices more easily and faster. One of these might be the 'availability bias', which forces you to rely on the most easily recalled information, rather than all available facts.

For example, when you go to buy a new mobile phone, you see two models: one from a popular brand, which is more expensive, and you've heard good things about it; and one from a lesser-known brand, which is cheaper but has fewer reviews and mixed feedback. You might lean towards the popular brand simply because you can easily recall positive information about it, even though you don't have all the facts. It also pushes you to ignore the possibility that the cheaper brand might be just as good or even better for your needs.

Similarly, confirmation biases might cause you to focus only on reviews that support your preference for a particular brand, while dismissing the feedback on the other. These shortcuts in thinking happen because your brain wants to make a quick decision, especially when the information is incomplete or conflicting.

How do you overcome these biases? Take a step back and ask yourself, 'Am I choosing this because it's truly the best option for me, or just because my brain is making a snap judgement?' Doing this will help you slow down and consider all the information more carefully, even under pressure. As a result, you're more likely to make a rational, well-informed choice instead of relying on mental shortcuts that can lead to less-than-ideal decisions.

Overconfidence bias

If you're not careful, overconfidence in your abilities can lead to overestimating your knowledge, underestimating risks and making decisions without considering alternative possibilities or seeking additional information. For example, in every kidnapping case I worked on, I was supported by a highly experienced team that would probe and test my suggested negotiation strategy – the last thing I wanted was to be overconfident and underestimate the situation or the kidnappers, even if I'd dealt with the same group many times previously. Collaborative decision-making within the CMT also reduced the chances of this bias occurring.

In the workplace, this might look like you asking one of your favourite team members to run a complex project with a tight deadline. They might have led similar projects in the past, yet because of overconfidence bias, you overlook red flags or warning signs and are overconfident in their ability. For example, you might focus on their successes while downplaying evidence of significant mistakes, previously missed deadlines or lower-quality work; 'Oh, that was just a one-off issue.' Doing so could also harm team morale due to perceived favouritism.

In another situation you may be convinced that a particular strategy will solve a problem, yet you still choose to seek input from your team. However, you end up only focusing on comments supporting your idea while disregarding valid concerns raised by others. You may even end up dismissing any dissenting view as 'overly negative' or 'not relevant', as well as dismissing any input completely from more junior or less experienced colleagues.

Framing effect

This is a form of cognitive bias that affects how we make decisions based on how information is presented, rather than the information itself. The same facts can lead to different choices depending on whether they're framed in a positive or negative light. For example, a weather forecast will often be presented as a 30 per cent chance of rain rather than a 70 per cent chance of sunshine.

Loss aversion

Human beings are hard-wired to avoid losses rather than pursue gains, even when both values are the same. For example, you will do more to prevent losing £100 than to gain £100. This bias can lead to overly cautious decisions and missed opportunities. For example, if I was hesitant to negotiate with kidnappers because I felt it might encourage further abductions, this might unwittingly bring about such an outcome due to this bias.

Sunk cost fallacy

This is the inclination to continue investing in a course of action or project because of the resources (time, money, effort) you have already invested, regardless of its prospects of succeeding.. It can lead to irrational decisions and a failure to objectively assess whether to continue or cut your losses.

Being aware of these strategies and acknowledging your biases will enable you to make better decisions and make more rational choices when it counts, particularly when you are faced with incomplete or conflicting information and are under pressure.

How can you enhance your decision-making even further?

- Seek out diverse perspectives and consider alternative viewpoints.
- Be aware of personal biases and consciously challenge preconceived notions. As a leader this might look like encouraging 'healthy dissent', such as inviting staff to come up with reasons why your idea won't work (e.g. playing devil's advocate).
- Consider additional information, particularly when facing incomplete or conflicting data.
- Reflect and deliberate on decisions (when you can) rather than making knee-jerk reactions. Trust your intuition yet seek clarification.

DEALING WITH DIFFICULT PEOPLE

Relationships magnify the human experience, whether for good or ill. Human beings are social creatures by nature and your interactions with others profoundly affect all aspects of your life, including our well-being. This is why increasing your understanding of human dynamics can help you achieve success when you are facing adversity and dealing with difficult people. The quality of your life depends on the quality of your relationships.

Research by the Mental Health Foundation revealed that people who are more socially connected to family, friends or their community are happier, physically healthier and live longer, with fewer mental health problems than people who are less well connected. It's also worth noting that it's not just the number of friends you have or whether you're in a committed relationship that matters, but the quality of your close relationships. Living in conflict or within a toxic relationship is more damaging than being alone.

According to the US Center for Disease Control and Prevention (CDC), socially connected people with stable and supportive relationships are more likely to make healthy choices and have better mental and physical health. They are also better able to cope with hard times, stress, anxiety and depression.

Positive interactions, such as expressing love, kindness and empathy, can foster positive emotions and boost mood. Conversely, negative interactions, such as conflict, criticism and rejection, can lead to stress, anxiety and negative emotions. These emotions usually arise when dealing with difficult people at home or in the workplace. Let's look at some practical skills for communicating with such people, establishing healthy boundaries and cultivating supportive networks in the workplace before, during and after times of crisis and adversity.

According to Katie Shonk, a research associate for Harvard Business School, some managers have had trouble with employees who entered the workforce during the Covid-19 pandemic. Shonk argues that when considering how to manage difficult staff, leaders often resort to generational stereotypes, both positive and negative.

- **Baby boomers (born 1946–64)**: are often characterised as self-absorbed and technophobic but hardworking.

- **Generation X (born 1965–80)**: is often viewed as independent but disengaged.

- **Millennials (born 1981–96)**: have been stereotyped as tech-savvy and ambitious but less loyal to employers.

The newest generation to start entering the workforce, Generation Z (born between 1997 and 2012), is receiving its own tough feedback. In June 2023, the online CV builder ResumeBuilder.com surveyed 1,344 managers and business leaders about their perceptions of Gen Z employees, and the results showed room for improvement. Of those surveyed, 74 per cent said they found these younger employees more challenging to work with than their older colleagues. Among the respondents, 49 per cent said they found it challenging to work with Gen Z all or most of the time.

These critiques were attributed to perceptions that Gen Z workers lack technological skills (39 per cent of those surveyed), effort (37 per cent) and motivation (37 per cent). Some surveyed also critiqued Gen Zers' communication skills and said they were overly sensitive to constructive feedback. On the plus side, some managers praised Gen Z workers as innovative and adaptable, and said they appreciated these employees' prioritisation on things such as Corporate Social Responsibility etc.

If some employees from Generation Z fall short of older colleagues on certain desired professional traits, this may reflect a couple of realities. Most notably, many members of Gen Z entered the workforce during the Covid-19 pandemic and may have been trained and started working remotely.

As such, they lacked face time and human contact at the beginning of their careers, which included learning the critical skills of team interaction and giving and receiving positive feedback and criticism. They also may have had less oversight and fewer encounters with colleagues, including valuable rapport-building interactions. Leaders wondering how to manage difficult staff should consider that the most common issue newcomers face is one that inevitably resolves over time: inexperience.

Managing difficult staff

If you're trying to figure out how to manage difficult staff, regardless of which generation or culture they belong to, Shonk provides the following suggestions:

- **Give them the training they need.** Shortcomings you perceive in your staff, such as lack of effort or weak communication skills, may result mainly from inadequate training. This is why they need training that focuses on building communication and conflict-resolution skills, which will help manage difficult conversations and promote a more robust and healthier organisation.

- **Avoid overgeneralising.** When dealing with difficult staff, we often fall back on generational stereotypes. In doing so, we risk marginalising and overlooking certain employees simply because of their age.

- **Try reverse mentoring.** This is where you have senior employees learn from junior ones through formal mentorship programmes. A primary goal is for employees to educate leaders about the challenges they and others may face in moving up the corporate ladder. It can also be a helpful way to foster productive yet difficult conversations among employees from different generations and levels of experience. It's just one way of highlighting that we all bring valuable expertise and knowledge to our organisations.

CASE STUDY #2

A mid-sized software development company faced a critical situation: a major client discovered a security vulnerability in their recently launched product. If not resolved within forty-eight hours, the client threatened to terminate the contract, risking the company's reputation and a loss of significant revenue. The CISO immediately convened a Crisis Management Team (CMT) composed of key decision-makers and those with relevant experience. These included:

- **Alex (senior developer, 20 years of experience):** Expert in legacy systems.
- **Riya (junior developer, 3 years of experience):** Skilled in the latest programming languages and agile methodologies.
- **Marcus (operations manager, 17 years of experience):** Strong in coordination of resources.
- **Steven (deputy general counsel, 14 years of experience):** Highly knowledgeable on legal issues as they relate to cyber-security.
- **Claire (communications manager, 7 years of experience).** Well thought of and capable crisis communications expert.

The initial response to the crisis was chaotic, with team members attempting to juggle multiple tasks at once, resorting to ineffective firefighting tactics. Marcus suggested dividing responsibilities, with each member focused on a specific task:

- Alex analysed the legacy code to identify the vulnerability's origin.
- Riya ran simulations to test potential patches.
- Marcus coordinated timelines and ensured everyone had the resources needed to fulfil their roles.

- Steven reviewed the immediate legal consequences along with any mandatory steps or notifications the company needed to make.
- Claire drafted a clear and concise statement ready to be published.

Eliminating the multitasking enabled each team member to dedicate their full attention to what they needed to do and not get distracted by the noise of seemingly urgent but not important tasks.

The team initially leaned on senior colleagues overlooking the perspectives of more junior members. Alex decided to encourage Riya to share her ideas. It was her familiarity with the latest debugging tools that led them to develop a workable solution.

The team also initially assumed that the issue stemmed from a common vulnerability based on experience, leading to wasted time investigating the wrong areas. Thankfully, it was a junior member of the team who made a comment in passing about how it would be worthwhile not to accept this initial assessment blindly, and to challenge assumptions. The CISO agreed to a quick, yet systematic, review of the entire system, avoiding assumptions or 'rules of thumb'.

The CMT worked collaboratively, resolving the issue within thirty-six hours. Thankfully, the vulnerability was traced to an overlooked feature in a recent update, something that wouldn't have been identified had the team relied on heuristic shortcuts.

The client was impressed by the team's transparent communication and efficiency, which in turn strengthened the business relationship. Additionally, the organisation developed a new crisis management protocol based on lessons learned.

KEY TAKEAWAYS FROM THIS CASE STUDY:

1. **Avoid Multitasking**: Assign focused roles during crises to optimise productivity.

2. **Leverage Variety**: A mix of skills, experiences and perspectives can lead to better solutions.

3. **Challenge Heuristics**: Avoid over-relying on past experiences; systematically analyse the problem.

4. **Strong Communication**: Clear and transparent messaging can strengthen team morale and confidence.

SUMMARY

In this chapter, we explored the skills you need to face and resolve conflicts and crises in both your personal and professional life. The key to succeeding lies in building emotional resilience, staying focused and learning to act with intention, even when uncertainty looms. Your ability to handle adversity directly influences the quality of your life, so mastering these techniques is crucial.

Crises come in all shapes and sizes, from daily frustrations to major life events. Rather than fearing them, this chapter has hopefully encouraged you to view these challenges as opportunities for growth. Whether you're negotiating high-stakes situations or handling workplace tensions consider the following strategies.

Practical Steps for Conflict Resolution:

1. **Form a Crisis Management Team (CMT)**: Don't go it alone – engage trusted advisors or colleagues who can offer support and perspective, and help you navigate tough situations.

2. **Control the narrative**: Clear communication is essential. The 'clean phone' concept recommends carefully managing what information is shared and how, ensuring one consistent message is communicated to prevent misunderstandings or an escalation of conflict.

3. **Active listening**: Listening deeply builds trust and rapport, forming the foundation for any successful resolution.

4. **Embrace patience and calm**: Rarely does rushing into a decision or acting rashly result in a great outcome. It often leads to mistakes instead. Patience and a calm demeanour allow for emotions to settle and even better answers to emerge.

5. **Adaptability**: Conflicts can shift unexpectedly. Being flexible and open to adjusting your approach increases your chances of successfully resolving conflict and tension.

6. **Preparation**: Before tackling difficult conversations, prepare your strategy, set boundaries and anticipate potential challenges.

Whether you're facing challenges at home or at work, active listening, clear and respectful communication, and thoughtful collaboration are key to resolving even the toughest conflicts. This chapter has also emphasised the importance of dealing with virtual conflicts in person, where possible, as impersonal emails or text messages can often make matters worse.

Building strong, positive relationships is essential for personal and professional success. Research shows that those with healthy, supportive connections tend to be happier, healthier and more resilient in times of stress. However, difficult people can strain these relationships. We've explored how improving communication and understanding is the key to navigating challenging interactions and fostering positive environments.

When managing difficult staff or colleagues, avoid relying on generational stereotypes. Instead, focus on proper training, constructive feedback and creating opportunities for employees to learn from each other through techniques like reverse mentoring. Often by flowing with the situation rather than trying to force a particular outcome at all costs, you can handle conflicts with far more grace and ease.

Making good decisions in bad situations takes consistent effort and practice. Obstacles such as cognitive biases, overconfidence, framing effects and the sunk cost fallacy can all hinder your ability to make good choices. However, by recognising and challenging these biases, you can make more informed, thoughtful decisions.

This chapter also emphasised the importance of slowing down, reflecting and seeking diverse perspectives. Instead of rushing into decisions or relying on mental shortcuts, you're invited to carefully consider all available information and explore alternative viewpoints. By doing so you can enhance your decision-making skills, especially when faced with incomplete or conflicting data.

As you continue to work your way through this book, you're gradually stacking proven tools and techniques that will sharpen your decision-making and relationship management skills, helping you navigate both personal and professional challenges more effectively. Some are likely to resonate with you and work more effectively than others – and that's OK. Take what works and discard what doesn't.

KEY TAKEAWAYS

1. **Comfort in discomfort**: Facing difficult conversations regularly builds resilience.
2. **Tackle problems head-on**: Avoiding issues only prolongs the discomfort.
3. **Trust your intuition**: Listen to your instincts when something feels off.
4. **Endure challenges**: Leadership in crises requires patience and persistence.

9

Embrace the Truth

A bitter truth is better than a sweet lie.

Unknown.

What we'll cover:

- **Moral and physical courage**
- **The mirror never lies test**
- **Slow down to speed up**
- **Skills for cultivating inner strength**

Whenever I give an interview or after I've delivered a keynote talk, the two questions I get asked most often are, 'What can I do to make sure I win every negotiation?', followed by, 'How do you stay calm when dealing with kidnappers and not let the pressure get to you?' Firstly, it depends on how you define 'winning'. If you're wondering, what are the top three things I can say that will guarantee me to win the deal, save lots of money on my rent or get this person to do what I want them to, no matter what? You're probably asking the wrong question. I'll explain why in a moment.

Secondly, regardless of how overwhelmed or uncertain I may have felt in such life-or-death situations, people invariably want to hear about some daring, high-stakes confrontation that went wrong. Yet the answer to both questions relies on one thing: courage – the moral and physical kind that makes me think, say and do the right thing even when it's hard.

Poor decision-making has led to countless scandals all over the world. These include the accounting irregularities of Enron in 2001, the banking practices of Lehman Brothers around the financial crisis of 2008, the Deepwater Horizon oil spillage involving BP in 2010, the 2015 Volkswagen (VW) emissions cheating, and Facebook in 2020 when it suppressed any opinion on its platform that was contrary to the official narrative of the US government during the Covid epidemic. Such decisions can all be attributed to a lack of courage in leadership. A lack of courage to think, feel and do the right thing, however difficult it may have been at the time.

MORAL AND PHYSICAL COURAGE

History is also littered with examples where a lack of moral courage resulted in intolerance to any view that didn't fit in with the mainstream. This has led to the rise of totalitarianism and dictatorships, with catastrophic consequences. We can see that today, as few leaders are willing to debate contentious topics such as climate, gender or immigration in a healthy, considerate manner, particularly with those who might hold a different opinion. It's so much easier, as a collective, to embrace victimhood and blame, and focus more on shouting rather than listening. This has led to the prevalence of cancel culture and de-platforming, both of which threaten the concept of freedom of speech, an essential pillar of democracy.

As a species, though, we are highly adaptable and resilient, having survived many extreme challenges during our evolution. We're all direct descendants of people who survived the most recent ice age, which lasted until approximately 10,000 years ago. We were able to endure for many reasons, not least because we developed complex social communities that relied on effective communication between one another. By doing so, our ancestors shared ideas and developed innovative solutions to their problems. They invented and used specialised tools, and developed a social identity that required them to work together to survive.

Why does this matter now and how can it help us as we face life's challenges? The ultimate test of moral and physical courage is knowing the right questions to ask, or the most appropriate decisions to make, or actions to take in any given moment. In my case, that might mean confronting kidnappers who are threatening to harm the hostages unless we pay them what they're demanding. I would in no uncertain terms remind them that the safety and welfare of the hostages rests solely with them.

What does courage have to do with embracing the truth? There is only ever one version of *the* truth, which is something that is universally true. It does not need agreement for it to survive, and it exists independent of people's belief systems. For example: gravity, night follows day, compound interest and, of course, the most important truth of all: the right way to make a cup of tea (milk or water in first).

However, this is not the same as when people talk about *their* truth, which is really just their opinion on a topic, nothing more. But many associate this opinion with their identity and make it as resolute as inviolable laws of nature. When this happens, there is no room for courage and certainly none for embracing what is universally true, such as putting milk in first if pouring from a teapot, otherwise water first if making tea in the cup. This is non-negotiable!

You'll hear those who engage in this kind of behaviour say something like it's what feels true to them, which is purely based on their individual experience and supports their view of the world. It could be argued that this is nothing more than a substitute for an inflated and non-negotiable opinion. This is why ideologies, by their very nature, can be dangerous, unyielding and divisive, for example, socialism, communism and fascism. These ideologies often demand that everyone follows the same beliefs, and anyone who disagrees is seen as an enemy. Even in smaller, everyday situations, ideologies can cause problems. Think about recent debates over topics like climate change or vaccinations. People with strong beliefs on either side can become so set in their ways that they refuse to listen to new information or other perspectives. As we've seen, this can lead to arguments, mistrust and even division among families, friends and communities.

Of course, there is nothing necessarily wrong with the substance of a person's self-declared 'truth' – that's the beauty of living in a free society; you can think and feel whatever it is you want to even if it's considered anathema, offensive or simply bizarre to others. However, those who espouse 'their truth' are usually unwilling or unable to countenance others doing the same; specifically, if it happens to be something they disagree with.

THE MIRROR NEVER LIES TEST

The importance of self-reflection, courage and living in alignment with one's values is nothing new. It was espoused by Plato in 400 BC, as well as by modern-day thinkers and commentators such as Brené Brown and Jordan Peterson.

How can we develop the courage to look adversity directly in the eye and overcome it with ease? I discovered a powerful way that has worked for me. Every single day I undertake what I call the 'mirror test'. I do my best to pass it, but some days I fail. How does it work? At the end of each day, before you go to sleep – especially if you've had an emotional conversation, had to make a difficult decision or overcome a challenging situation – look in the mirror and be completely honest with yourself, taking stock of your thoughts, feelings and behaviours from the day.

There can be no hiding place because the mirror never lies. Ask yourself what your intention was. Did you do everything to communicate as effectively as possible? Did you have that difficult conversation? How did you get on? Did you make the best possible decision you could, based on the best possible information you had at the time? Not in some Machiavellian or manipulative way in order for you to win at someone else's expense, but with genuine openness, curiosity and, most importantly, zero judgement. Why? Because the two golden rules of all successful communication are:

#1 IT'S NOT ABOUT YOU

#2 FIRST SEEK TO UNDERSTAND, BEFORE BEING UNDERSTOOD

You can B.S. everyone else about how great you were or how righteous your viewpoint is, but you can't lie to yourself indefinitely. This is why you need to take the 'mirror never lies test' regularly. It develops integrity that will free you from the inner conflict you carry around all day. It helps you develop honesty about your intentions and motivations. It exposes inconsistencies in your thoughts, words and behaviour.

Remember, this is not about you overcompensating and becoming either a ball-buster or a wimp. Far from it. It's a means of checking the depth of your presence and how well you really know yourself; beneath the surface and behind the various masks you wear when facing the world.

Consider asking yourself the following questions when taking the test:

1. How did I do today?
2. What was my intention? Was it the right one?
3. What's the real issue here?
4. Is that the *real* issue?
5. Am I being hypocritical or self-centred?
6. Do I need to change my behaviour or the story I'm telling myself about x, y, z?
7. How could I conduct myself with more integrity?

SLOW DOWN TO SPEED UP

It is difficult to identify and fully embrace the truth when you're pushing through your day, ticking things off your to-do list and being buffeted around by the vagaries of life. Without slowing down and adopting a broader perspective, even well-intentioned decisions can lead to unintended or negative consequences. We might find ourselves succumbing to a 'fool's gold of truth', mistaking something that appears true or good at first glance for something genuinely valuable or correct, largely due to being hasty in our judgement or focusing too narrowly on something.

For example, you decide to stay on at work to finish a project and as a result miss your kid's school play or swimming gala. This might be good for your career but less so for your relationship with your kids. Or you may decide to introduce cost-cutting measures in your business by outsourcing the customer service function, usually overseas. While this is likely to reduce costs, it may ultimately lead to poor customer experiences (as anyone who has ever tried to phone a customer service number can relate to), as well as long-term brand damage.

Practical steps to avoid a fool's gold of truth

1. **Slow down:** Slowing down can improve emotional awareness. It also creates space to review and reflect, thereby reducing the risk of impulsive decision-making driven by stress, ego or other external pressures.
2. **Pause and reflect:** Build a habit of asking, 'What might I be missing?' or 'What are the potential consequences of this decision and how might we mitigate them?'
3. **Use the premortem technique:** In order to identify and highlight hidden risks, imagine your decision failing and consider why it might have happened.
4. **Seek diverse perspectives:** Taking time allows leaders to gather feedback from people with different perspectives and experiences to challenge assumptions, reduce blind spots and reveal better alternatives.

> **5. Scenario planning:** Consider not just the desired outcome but also possible unintended consequences.

Good intentions don't necessarily guarantee good outcomes. Without slowing down and expanding your awareness, you risk mistaking an appealing but flawed option (i.e. 'fool's gold') for genuine truth, leading to decisions that may harm you, your teams or your goals in ways you hadn't expected.

This is why having the courage to do the right thing is crucial. The criteria for this will be your values and beliefs, which in turn influence whether you pass the mirror test. This will also guide you when the consequences of your decisions begin to bite.

Power of the pause

Before taking the mirror test, it's worth pausing to give you time to clear your mind and let go of the stress or worries from the day and focus on what's happening for you right now. This pause can also be done throughout your day. It's simply about taking a short break to think before reacting or moving on to the next task. Consider it a 'tactical mental reset' between activities. It enables you to calm down, think clearly and decide how to respond instead of rushing into things.

> **During the day, if you feel you're about to lose your patience or things feel like they're getting out of control:**
>
> Pause for ten to thirty seconds and notice whatever is showing up for you, either mentally, emotionally or physically.

Take several slow, deep breaths, exhaling fully each time. Be completely aware of each one.

Once you're feeling calmer, choose how you're going to respond rather than react. A powerful question you can ask yourself before choosing your response is: 'Will this bother me when I'm aged ninety?' 'If not, why let it bother me now!'

Find the lesson

By pausing regularly, you can realise that life is happening in your favour, even when it might not feel like it. Every event in your life can teach you something if you allow it to. Those who insist on blaming their circumstances on others and dwell in a victim or entitled mentality will fail and continue to suffer. This is key to overcoming adversity.

When I found out my mum had taken her own life, I took my grief and turned it into anger against the world, including those who I felt weren't there for me when I needed them the most. Not long afterwards, I found myself sitting on a bare kitchen floor in a small flat with no furniture, feeling very sorry for myself, having also just gone through an acrimonious divorce. If there had been a world championship for blaming others, I would've been a serious contender for the title!

However, I paused and took my first ever mirror test. Inevitably, I failed. But then the truth became clear (as opposed to some nebulous version of 'my truth'): no matter what I thought, felt or did, nothing would ever bring her back.

As I wrote in the introduction to this book, this insight meant I had complete agency and responsibility for what I thought, felt and did next. It's a point I return to again and again, because it's one of the main lessons I hope you take from reading this, and that you apply it to your own life.

At that moment, while I was staring into the mirror, I decided that this tragedy wouldn't be in vain. I would learn from what I had experienced and live a life focusing on informing, inspiring, enabling and helping others.

Your past is only your future if you go back there. So, utilise your positive experiences while letting go of the negative. Everyone has faced challenges, failures and setbacks, and we've all experienced pain and loss to varying degrees. The difference between those who become successful and those who give up is the ability to find the lesson in failure. The successful ones come up with a new, more empowering meaning, and use this unique perspective to keep going and not allow the past to define them.

Over time, I discovered that life is one big negotiation that is constantly teaching me tools, techniques and insights. By applying them consistently, I've been able to become a more effective communicator, make better decisions and find a centred calmness when I face stress or overwhelm. You too can experience this. It won't always be plain sailing and mistakes are inevitable. Yet dwelling on such mistakes diverts your precious time, focus and energy away from making real progress.

SKILLS FOR CULTIVATING INNER STRENGTH

The process of overcoming adversity should begin before the challenging situation even occurs. Train your brain to be resilient by building your inner strength and developing a growth mindset. For example, reframe the meaning you give your experiences, embracing more ease, virtue and compassion in your life, as well as committing to zero negativity (no matter what). Examine your limiting beliefs to uncover what's holding you back. Develop a support system that you can fall back on, and when the time comes to dig deep and work out how you're going to overcome whatever adversity you are faced with, you'll be prepared. Lean into the work that you've already done and use your inner strength to handle the situation.

Resilience comes from inner strength. It is a deep, unstoppable belief in yourself and your ability to overcome obstacles and bounce back from failures and challenges. It doesn't depend on the actions of anyone else or on your circumstances. But many people have a vague concept of inner strength but haven't pinpointed a precise definition.

This is probably because inner strength is a concept open to interpretation. Psychologists use the term 'inner strength' to refer loosely to the wide range of mental and emotional resources (behaviours, skills and attitudes) that keep us stable and adaptable. The following are the internal resources every human being has that allow them to adapt, change and bounce back from adversity. Focusing on them will help you discover that you're stronger than you realise:

Adaptive emotional skills: Mindfulness, resilience, empathy
Positive emotions: Love, self-compassion, gratitude
Optimistic outlook: Confidence, openness, determination
Engaged manner: Relaxed, humorous, takes responsibility
Warm personality: Generous, hard-working, wise

Many of these aren't innate personality traits but skills you can develop with practice. For example, gratitude, confidence or empathy, which will lead to a more fulfilled and joyful life.

Engaging in activities that promote resilience can help you cope better with adversity. These include visualisation, mindfulness, journalling, exercise and creative hobbies. Such activities foster a positive mindset, build self-confidence and provide a sense of purpose and fulfilment.

Here are more ways you can cultivate your inner strength:

Find comfort in discomfort

Embracing things that create uneasiness is essential to expanding your sphere of comfort. Take care of your physical and mental well-being by getting enough rest, eating nutritious meals and engaging in activities that help you relax and recharge. Self-care is essential for maintaining mental clarity and emotional stability. Successful people who can thrive regardless of circumstances prioritise their routines, rituals and habits. It's not that they have more time in the day; they use it more wisely by building empowering habits. When tough times hit, it can feel like your life is out of control. Stop yourself from spiralling by staying disciplined and establishing routines and rituals that work.

My three Ms morning routine

Earlier, I provided my evening routine that helps me unwind and get a decent night's sleep, irrespective of whatever challenges I've had to deal with during the day. Here is my morning routine that I follow, again aiming for 80 per cent of the time. There is sufficient flexibility with these three elements that it doesn't matter where in the world I am or how much time I have, I can still do them. On some days I'll spend literally one minute on each, whereas on others it may be thirty minutes or more.

The key point to my three Ms (or indeed any routine) is that it's not meant to be just another thing to tick off your achiever's checklist. If it turns into a chore or you become stressed because you miss a day, you might need to rethink the intention behind why you're doing it. Yes, a routine that you stick to can really help you get more stuff done while enjoying the process, but if you find yourself treating it as just some productivity hack, you're missing the point.

Movement
I start with moving my body. This could be anything from ten minutes of stretching, yoga, or mobility work through to an hour's walk, run or gym session.

Meditation
Usually I aim for twenty minutes, but it could be just two or three, where I simply just sit still and focus on my breathing. I sometimes combine this with going for a walk.

Mindset
Filling my mind at the start of each day with something positive, useful or enjoyable helps set the tone for the day. This might involve reading a book or an article, listening to a podcast or some music, or perhaps writing something.

Other suggestions include:

Work on your skills
People who are good at what they do share a similar trait, regardless of what they excel at. They all put in the time to improve their skills and take their talents to the next level. Such people know there is always room for improvement.

Emotional regulation

Maintaining emotional composure and regulating your emotions are crucial in tense situations. In the world of hostage negotiations, remaining calm, composed and focused allows negotiators to think clearly. It helps them make rational decisions. Emotional regulation techniques like deep breathing and mindfulness can help manage stress. They also help you maintain control in high-pressure situations.

Mental rehearsal

By imagining the different and challenging scenarios you're likely to face, including those all-important conversations, you can mentally rehearse your responses, visualising yourself staying calm, using effective communication and achieving positive outcomes.

Positive self-talk

Cultivating positive self-talk can help you maintain confidence, resilience and a solution-oriented mindset during negotiations. Remind yourself of your strengths, capabilities and progress.

CASE STUDY #1

A large financial consulting firm faced a critical issue with an upcoming client presentation. Gary, a senior consultant, firmly believed that the analysis he had prepared for a major client was flawless. He had spent weeks working on the report, conducting thorough research and drawing on his years of experience. When a few team members raised concerns about some of the financial projections, he felt aggrieved and immediately dismissed them. His colleagues reiterated their concerns and said they felt Gary was overreacting and being unreasonable. Gary asserted himself as he was prone to do and stood by the accuracy of his report.

To Gary, the concerns raised by his colleagues were minor and due to their inexperience. In his eyes, the report was sound, and he didn't take kindly to his 'model of the world' being challenged. He pushed forward with the presentation plan. However, during a final review by the managing partner, several critical errors in the projections were identified. The financial model was built on outdated market assumptions, which could have led to disastrous recommendations for the client if presented.

The reality – the objective truth – was that the report was flawed, no matter how strongly Gary believed otherwise. His 'truth' was rooted in personal conviction and experience, but that could not change the fact that the data was inaccurate. The firm had to rush to fix the errors and adjust the presentation at the last minute, saving the relationship with the client but creating unnecessary stress for the entire team.

This situation underscores a common challenge in professional environments: the tension between personal perspective and objective truth. Gary's 'truth' was shaped by his inflexible view of the world as well as his own flaws. It wasn't grounded in the facts. The truth – the accuracy of financial projections, based on reliable and current data – was not subjective and could not be bent to fit personal beliefs. The lesson here is clear: while everyone has their own viewpoint, relying on objective facts and truth is essential.

SUMMARY

Taking the time to train your mind and slow down before you act will enable you to develop a more open attitude and flexible perspective, rather than adhering to rigid dogma. This requires courage. With practice over time, you can train yourself to operate from a place of equanimity where you are not easily ruffled or triggered.

This includes your ability to accept and acknowledge that other people will have different opinions and beliefs to you – and that's OK. If you are more flexible and open to alternative points of view, it releases the tight grip with which you are holding your so-called 'truths' and realise that other people's views are just as valid. This doesn't mean you can't stand up for a cause you believe in or against an injustice that needs addressing; it simply means that the beliefs you hold aren't cast in stone nor are they necessarily linked to your identity. You can listen and engage with other opinions in a way that doesn't treat them as a threat to your very existence. Not only will this improve your decision-making, it brings forth more harmony and less division in a world that is desperate for both.

Imagine if schools taught kids how the mind works and the ways in which they can harness their own inner game to experience healthy thoughts and positive emotions and ultimately engage in better behaviour. If they did, I think it's fair to say that there would likely be fewer mental health issues in society. If we can ultimately tame our minds, it will enable us to communicate with others in a far more humane and compassionate way.

KEY TAKEAWAYS

1. Catch and replace ALL negative self-talk with empowering beliefs that help you develop courage. The more you shift yourself towards a positive mindset, the more equipped you will be to deal with whatever shows up.
2. Slow down and stay focused on what you can control. Set realistic yet challenging goals, and build consistent habits to see you through to the finish line.
3. Cultivate inner strength by expanding your threshold of tolerance. Learn how to think, feel and act appropriately in ever-increasing levels of adversity. Hope for the best, while planning for the worst.

PART FOUR

WORKING
WITH OTHERS

Success Is a Team Sport

'Teamwork is the ability to work together towards a common vision. It is the fuel that allows common people to attain uncommon results.'

Andrew Carnegie

What we'll cover:

- **Building bridges: Seek cooperation and collaboration**
- **Hire for attitude, train for skill**
- **Locate your exit: When to stay and when to walk away**

In moments of adversity, your ability to think, feel and act calmly and wisely is tested. But maintaining composure and making rational decisions is paramount to overcoming obstacles. You can cultivate this skill set through experience, reflection and, above all, practice. However, extending this ability beyond the decisions you make as an individual to collaborate effectively with others requires a more nuanced approach. Part of the nuance lies in the fact that human beings are neurologically driven to want to feel connected and valued. This approach also requires empathy, effective communication, a solutions-oriented mindset, resilience and strong leadership. By cultivating these qualities within your team and fostering a collaborative environment built on trust, respect and mutual support, you can navigate through adversity with grace and emerge stronger together.

First and foremost, fostering a culture of empathy lays the foundation for collaborative success. Understanding the perspectives, emotions and motivations of those we work with builds bridges between us and allows for more meaningful interactions. By acknowledging and validating the feelings of others (even if we disagree with them), we also create an environment that promotes better communication and fosters a sense of camaraderie, making it easier to navigate turbulent times together. This is made easier by ensuring that the people you bring onto your team have the right attitude. You can always train them on the skills they need. After all, no one wants to work with a highly talented diva or jerk!

Clear and transparent communication is also essential for working harmoniously with others. As we discovered in previous chapters, active listening involves hearing another person's words and understanding their underlying emotions and concerns. It's important to express oneself honestly and openly, while also actively listening to the viewpoints of others.

Maintaining a solutions-oriented mindset is another crucial aspect of working with others in difficult situations. Instead of dwelling on problems or assigning blame, focus on finding viable solutions and moving forward. This requires a willingness to adapt, innovate and remain flexible in uncertainty. Collaborative problem-solving encourages diverse perspectives and allows the exploration of creative solutions that may not have been apparent initially.

Furthermore, cultivating resilience individually and as a team is essential for effectively navigating adversity. Resilience enables us to bounce back from setbacks and persevere when we face challenges. By fostering a culture of resilience within a team, we empower each other to overcome obstacles and grow stronger together. This can involve providing support, encouragement and resources to help team members cope and thrive in difficult circumstances. Despite your best efforts, sometimes certain challenges within a team mean you might have to let somebody go or even walk away yourself.

Lastly, effective leadership plays a pivotal role in guiding teams through adversity. People scrutinise their leaders to understand the implicit as well as explicit expectations, values and rules. This is why the best leaders lead by example, demonstrating composure, compassion and decisiveness in uncertainty. They provide direction, inspiration and support, rallying their team members towards a common goal. We know that emotions are contagious and that effective leaders are mindful of theirs. They foster trust and confidence within the team, instilling a sense of purpose and unity that propels them forward even in the most challenging times.

BUILDING BRIDGES: SEEK COOPERATION AND COLLABORATION

One of the primary objectives of effective communication is to bring about some form of cooperation or collaboration. Working with others to get the best out of them (and you) helps you increase your chances of getting through difficult times. It's what we would do all the time with kidnappers, as well as with the hostage's family. It's what you can do if you want to attract and retain clients, customers and colleagues who want to keep coming back for more.

I'm sure most of us have had to do business with people who seem to be hard work and require lots of effort to get along with. This is why we prefer doing business with people we like. It also enhances our ability to influence and persuade others if we have a likeable personality and behaviour. This is different to wanting others to like us. Be aware of the difference and avoid falling into the trap of seeking that external validation.

Support rather than shift the conversation

Jennie Jerome, an American socialite and the mother of Winston Churchill, reflected in her memoirs about dining separately with two of Britain's most formidable prime ministers, Benjamin Disraeli and William Gladstone, who were fierce political rivals.

After dining with Gladstone, she left convinced *he* was the most intelligent man in England. However, after sitting next to Disraeli, she walked away feeling like *she* was the cleverest woman in England. Disraeli, also Queen Victoria's favourite prime minister, had a unique gift: he knew how to guide a conversation by supporting, rather than shifting or dominating it.

In her book, *You're Not Listening: What You're Missing and Why It Matters*, Kate Murphy explains how the best listeners (and therefore the best communicators) always prioritise giving a supporting response rather than one designed to shift the conversation on to the other person or topic of their choosing. They acknowledge and evaluate, are genuinely curious and understand the other person's point of view rather than trying to sway it.

In the following example, notice how Jane tries to **shift** the conversation instead of supporting it. She redirects it towards her own experiences rather than focusing on Bill's feelings. While her communication is not inherently negative, it diverts attention from Bill, preventing him from fully sharing and working through the issue to find a solution.

Bill: I've been feeling overwhelmed at work lately. There's so much on my plate, and I'm struggling to balance it all.

Jane: Oh, I know exactly what you mean. My job has been crazy busy, too. I've been working late every night this week.

Bill: Yeah, it's tough. I try to prioritise, but there's always something urgent that throws me off.

Jane: Same here! Last Friday, I had this huge project dropped on me out of nowhere. I had to cancel my weekend plans just to catch up.

Bill: That sounds frustrating.

Jane: Yeah, it was. And the worst part is, I didn't even get a thank you for putting in all that extra time.

Now let's look at an example of how Jane **supports** the conversation by asking open-ended questions, validating Bill's feelings and focusing on his experience. Instead of shifting the topic to her own challenges or offering unsolicited advice, Jane stays present, allowing Bill to share more and feel understood. Naturally, once this has been done, Jane has earned the right to help Bill in coming up with solutions, but not before.

Bill: I've been feeling overwhelmed at work lately. There's so much on my plate, and I'm struggling to balance it all.

Jane: That sounds really stressful. It's hard when the workload starts piling up. How have you been managing so far?

Bill: Well, I try to prioritise, but there's always something urgent that throws me off.

Jane: I totally get that. It seems like no matter how well you plan, those last-minute things sneak in. What do you usually do when that happens?

Bill: I just push through, but it's exhausting.

Jane: I can imagine! It sounds like you're doing everything you can to stay on top of things. How do you relax after those tough days?

Rather than asserting your own thoughts or feelings on to a conversation to shift it, take the time and effort to support it instead. This is particularly powerful if you disagree with what the other person is saying. Just because you're supporting the conversation by validating and acknowledging what the other person is saying, it doesn't necessarily mean that you support or condone the actual words or sentiment. This is about building bridges and seeking some form of cooperation or collaboration where possible.

Avoid playing hard ball

Some people think that being tough is the way to succeed in life. We're not talking here about the mental or physical toughness that comes from forging resilience in difficult times or overcoming setbacks to win in sport, for example.

I'm referring to the ineffective hardball tactics used to bring about a win-lose outcome in daily life. You know the kind of people who do this. You may even work with some of them. Do they instil in you a desire to go above and beyond for them? Of course not.

In *Beyond Winning*, the authors describe various hardball tactics to watch out for, particularly in the workplace. All are driven by ego and emotion, which were also commonplace in many kidnap negotiations I dealt with. It's important to be familiar with these as they can directly impact the efficacy of your decision-making.

1. **Making an extreme demand before making gradual, small concessions.** This is a common technique that shields people against premature concessions. While this tactic may prevent quick deal closures, it can also potentially prolong conversations unnecessarily. To counteract this approach, you need to understand clearly what you're looking to get from the situation, know your boundaries (walk-away point) and resist being unsettled by someone else's belligerence or assertiveness.

2. **'My hands are tied' approach.** These may surface when the other person claims they have limited discretion. Verify the authenticity of their claims, as it may be necessary to engage with someone possessing greater authority to make a decision.

3. **Take it or leave it.** These kinds of offers are presented as non-negotiable and are generally discouraged. To defuse this tactic, focus on the offer's content and, where possible, respond with a counter-offer that addresses both parties' needs.

4. **Unreciprocated offers.** The other person requests that you back down or concede before they agree to something. Don't lower what you ask for too soon and show that you're open to alternatives.

5. **Personal insults and provocations.** These exploit your insecurities, making you vulnerable and are a favourite of emotional vampires. When faced with such attacks, take a break and communicate that you won't tolerate insults or other manipulative tactics.

6. **Bluffing, puffing and lying.** Exaggeration and misrepresentation of facts can make for weary and tiresome conversations. Approach claims that seem too good to be true with detached scepticism and, if required, clarify and verify with open and searching questions, which encourages reflection and elaboration without unnecessary confrontation. Such as, 'That's interesting. How did you come to that conclusion?' or 'What's a good example of that?'

7. **Threats and warnings.** Recognise them as such and consider calling them out. Like when dealing with children, never reward bad behaviour.

We've established the importance of building bridges and fostering cooperation with others by demonstrating an understanding of their perspectives, emotions and motivations, rather than adopting a win-at-all-costs, hardball approach. Let's move on to the importance of having the right attitude, rather than skills, in order to create the best team possible.

HIRE FOR ATTITUDE, TRAIN FOR SKILL

The mantra 'hire for attitude, train for skill' is well established in recruitment circles. It prioritises an individual's personal qualities, mindset and character over their technical competencies, because success is rarely a solo endeavour. What's needed is continuous and collaborative teamwork. Attitude is connected to being someone others can trust and working well with others.

What are the right attitudes to look for when you are establishing your team and, later on, when you're navigating the various storms you can expect to face? In my experience, they include positivity, empathy, gratitude, compassion, curiosity, adaptability, resilience and emotional self-regulation. These are particularly important qualities for your team to have when they are under pressure. Skills, on the other hand, can be cultivated through training.

An example of this in action is Google, which is known for valuing qualities like curiosity and a willingness to learn in its staff. The organisation understands that specific skills can evolve and be acquired on the job. However, having a passion for learning and a positive approach to problem-solving from the start is essential.

When I first meet the hostage's family or colleagues on a case, I must quickly decide who is best suited to join the CMT, the small group of trusted individuals who will make all the crucial decisions regarding the negotiations, including how much money we are willing and able to pay as a ransom. The group will also include the all-important communicator, who will be the person physically speaking with the kidnappers.

While language proficiency, accents and cultural nuances are a huge consideration, the main thing I look for is, 'Can I work with this person over a long period under the most intense pressure?' In other words, I'm looking for attitude, agreeableness and, of course, trust. I might also subtly steer initial conversations with them around any previous challenges, problem-solving or crises they've been involved in. Similar questions can easily form the basis of more mainstream interview processes within an organisation.

In a wider business context, hiring for attitude ensures alignment with the organisation's values and culture. Without such alignment, creating a cohesive and harmonious workplace is difficult.

How can you develop the right attitude in your organisation?

- Communicate your organisation's values and culture in job descriptions. Highlight qualities and attitudes that align with the team or company's ethos. An excellent example of this is the nutrition company, Huel, who's company slogan is 'Don't be a dick'.*
- Encourage open and transparent communication about the importance of attitude (over and above skill) in the hiring process.
- Incorporate behavioural questions during interviews and appraisals that elicit responses related to attitudes, such as how they handle challenges, work in teams or approach problem-solving.
- Leverage personality assessments to gauge a candidate's disposition and attitudes when compared alongside the role.

---

* The slogan 'Don't be a dick' encourages treating others with respect and decency. Similar in many ways to the New Zealand All Blacks rugby team's 'No dickheads' policy, which emphasised humility, teamwork and respect, Huel's take on it boils down to the following: **Show up** – be present and engaged in what you do; **Have integrity** – be honest and do the right thing; **Be authentic** – stay true to who you are, without pretending; **Take responsibility** – own up to your actions, both good and bad. **Be nice** – kindness goes a long way in making a positive environment; **Don't gossip** – avoid talking behind people's backs; **Be a team** – work together and support each other; **Help others** – offer a hand when someone needs it.

These tools can provide valuable insights into how individuals approach work and collaboration.

- Develop assessments that evaluate a candidate's alignment with the organisation's culture. This can include scenarios and questions related to the company's values.
- Design training programmes that address specific skill gaps.
- Implement mentorship programmes to pair new hires with experienced employees who can guide them in acquiring technical skills and assimilating into the organisational culture.

CASE STUDY #1

Southwest Airlines is known for its unique and successful approach to the airline industry, and attributes much of its success to hiring for attitude. Their employees are selected for their passion, positivity and dedication to providing exceptional customer service, which has contributed to Southwest's reputation as a customer-centric and employee-friendly airline. The result? For fifteen consecutive years, they have made *Fortune* magazine's list of 'World's Most Admired Companies', recognised as a 'Best Employer' by *Forbes*, as well as one of Glassdoor's 'Best Places to Work'.

Southwest set themselves apart from the competition by focusing on creating a culture that prioritises people – both employees and customers – and delivering exceptional service through compassion, teamwork and a unique attitude.

They focus on embodying three things:

1. **A warrior spirit** (being fearless in terms of delivering the service)
2. **A servant's heart** (treating others with respect and following the golden rule of team before self)
3. **A fun-loving attitude** (by not taking yourself too seriously)

Their approach also revolves around several key practices:

People-first culture

Southwest Airlines is known for its deep commitment to its employees, fostering an environment where they feel valued, supported and empowered. The 'warriors for love' genuinely care about their work and each other, creating a positive atmosphere that naturally extends to customers. This culture creates employees who are motivated to go the extra mile.

Hire for attitude, train for skill

Southwest Airlines emphasise hiring people with the right attitude – those who genuinely embody the values of teamwork and service – rather than focusing solely on technical skills. They also emphasise the importance of not being a jerk. Their philosophy is that skills can be taught, but a genuine, service-oriented attitude is harder to instil.

Empowerment and trust

Employees are given the autonomy to make decisions and act in the best interest of the customer. This empowerment fosters a sense of ownership, pride and reliability, allowing them to resolve issues creatively and with care. This trust is a key differentiator in the customer service experience, when compared to other airlines.

Fun and positivity

The company encourages a sense of fun in the workplace; for example, employees joking with passengers to create a relaxed, enjoyable atmosphere. This light-heartedness helps build rapport with customers and stands out in an industry often seen as rigid or impersonal.

Operational efficiency and customer care

While Southwest Airlines are operationally efficient (they are also at the time of writing the fourth largest commercial airline fleet in the world), their primary focus is always on the human element. This balance of efficiency and care sets them apart from competitors who might prioritise cost-cutting or automation over customer experience.

So, what can you learn and apply from Southwest's values and practices? Having the right people with the right attitude in your team, who are willing to embrace continuous learning and not take themselves too seriously (or, as is increasingly common these days, stuck in self-righteousness) is crucial, particularly when it comes to successfully navigating the constant change we all face every day.

As we've discovered, it's far easier to train people in a new skill rather than dealing with staff who moan and are reluctant to adapt, and who see change and progress as a threat.

LOCATE YOUR EXIT: WHEN TO STAY AND WHEN TO WALK AWAY

The French philosopher and playwright Jean-Paul Sartre famously wrote, 'Hell is other people.' Anyone who has had to deal with small team dynamics can readily attest to this sentiment: interpersonal relationships, particularly in confined or challenging situations, can be sources of intense difficulty and conflict. It's the same in our families and friendship groups – these close relationships can also be fraught with conflict, judgement and even anguish.

I experienced this first-hand when I was deployed overseas to Iraq as part of a small team to debrief and interrogate captured insurgents. We were a mix of backgrounds, ages and life experience. At first glance, we must have looked a right motley crew of renegades – young pups and old dogs not quite fitting in with any normal or recognised hierarchy. We were made up of young full-time military personnel from the Army, Navy and Air Force, along with older reservists, each with specialist skills and experience.

At the time, I was a serving Metropolitan Police Special Branch officer, based at Scotland Yard in London, working alongside the British Security Service, MI5, engaged in covert intelligence gathering and counter-terrorism operations. One morning, I was approached by a colleague I knew reasonably well who suggested we go to the local coffee shop next to St James's tube station. Over a couple of Americanos and pastel de nata pastries, he asked if I'd be interested in getting involved in a different type of intelligence work in addition to my day job.

This was not long after 9/11 and the UK, like a lot of countries at the time, was fighting a tidal wave of Islamist-inspired attacks by homegrown terrorists seeking to kill as many innocent people as they could on British streets. I said yes, and within a year I found myself thousands of miles from home in a low-rise building, positioned in a discreet corner of an airfield with the aforementioned motley crew.

For the first few months, we worked seamlessly together, gathering valuable intelligence. But gradually the cracks started to appear. The younger members of the team, used to a far more rigid and formal way of working, began to push back against our more relaxed, flexible and less deferential approach. Some had been part of the previous team we had replaced. In their minds, we'd never live up to their idealised version of the way things used to be. While they had the skills to get the job done, it became clear they didn't have the right mindset to thrive in this new, more fast-paced, high-pressured, uncertain, yet relaxed environment we were now in. Due to various political and operational pressures, the team was disbanded three months later.

Previously we discussed how in a kidnapping case, I would spend 80 per cent of my time managing the 'crisis within the crisis'. In other words, the internal politics, egos, silo thinking and conflicting demands of my own side, whether that be the hostage's employer, family or another stakeholder looking to have their say.

How can we utilise what we've learned throughout this book so far to navigate this relationship minefield? The first step is making sure you align with the other person before attempting to redirect them. This means acknowledging and reflecting the other person's perspective back to them, before you've earned the right to try to redirect them to where you want to steer the conversation; in other words, to change their mind or behaviour. For example, say you are an estate agent, and a potential buyer tells you how they don't really trust estate agents because they're just trying to sell any property to make a sale. Now, while you might consider this to be an unfair character assassination of your profession, there's no point in starting off the conversation trying to defend estate agents or, indeed, your own high standards by saying something along the lines of: 'Well, sir, I can assure you that we are not like that here. We are fully accredited and abide by a code of conduct and we only do . . . etc.'

Not a good move. First, you must align with them. Compare this passioned defence of your industry with the following: 'You're absolutely right, sir, some estate agents in the past have seriously undermined the professionalism and integrity of what we do. It sounds like you've had some bad experiences in the past. If so, I'm sorry to hear that.' Can you see the difference? In the second example, at no point did you try to convince the potential customer they are mistaken and that your integrity as an estate agent is above reproach (in other words, you aren't telling them that they're wrong!)

In a wider business context, you might choose to first align with your client or customer by saying something like: 'Is it OK if I share with you where I think you're at with this project?' Why? Because just like in the previous example, it enables you to achieve the Holy Grail of communicating, which is to make the other person feel seen, heard and understood.

Sometimes, despite your best intentions, the other person is not interested in making meaningful progress. Maybe they are not open to learning new ways of doing something, or the workplace culture doesn't align with your values. In such cases it's probably time to move on. Walking away from a deal, job or relationship is not a crime. What is criminal is that you take more time than you need to make this decision. If it or they don't value you, or aren't willing to do what is necessary, then it's time to move on. You owe yourself that.

Before you reach that point, consider the following steps to help you make the right decision about whether to stay or walk away.

1. **Evaluate the pros and cons:** Weigh the rewards (e.g., growth, achievement) against the pressures (e.g., stress, health impact).
2. **Reflect on your priorities:** Determine if the role aligns with your values and goals at this stage in your life.
3. **Explore solutions:** Can the challenges you face be mitigated through simple adjustments like workload changes or accessing support?
4. **Seek advice:** Discuss with mentors or trusted colleagues for additional perspectives (but don't take advice from someone who you wouldn't swap places with).
5. **Visualise the various scenarios:** Picture life one, five and ten years from now in all options, and identify which one resonates more. Are you able to rationalise it objectively, too? Balance logic and intuition, and take your time to decide thoughtfully.

Go for no (for now)

If you've decided to stay rather than walk away, you may still be facing a tense situation or other conflict that you'll need to deal with. Sometimes this means standing your ground and having a difficult conversation. To succeed at this, understanding how to say 'no' without actually using the word can help. To overcome the powerful, almost instinctive, urge to always say 'yes', or to agree to something you're uncomfortable with, take the time to pause, breathe and consider whether this is a moment to signal a 'no', at least for now.

Being able to say 'no' is a powerful skill for communication, conflict resolution and everyday situations. Rather than portraying you as being difficult or inflexible, saying 'no' without uttering the word can strengthen your position, allow you to set limits, communicate a clear sense of self-worth, protect priorities and establish clear boundaries. It also integrates into a healthy 'battle rhythm' by enabling you and others to work effectively for long periods, without becoming overwhelmed or exhausted by agreeing to take on too much.

This is something we used regularly in important negotiations and is a structured, consistent routine that helps teams stay organised and focused. It's a way to manage tasks and maintain clear communication, while balancing workloads effectively, preventing burnout and fostering mutual respect among team members. Something that was missing in my small-team dynamic experience mentioned earlier.

Why do we want to avoid using the 'no' word explicitly? Because it can shut down the conversation. By using qualifying questions or statements instead, we can still signal that we're not happy with an offer or a particular aspect of the deal.

For example, 'Your current offer is not enough to make this deal a viable option for us right now. I know that it's in both our interests, though, to reach an agreement on this.' Or: 'How can we solve this problem so that it works for both of us?'

Because all communication involves give and take (which is not the same as a compromise), indicating a 'no' is not rude, ungrateful or inflexible, but rather a deliberate decision to strengthen your position and act in your best interests. This is what we are doing in the examples above. Why do we want to do this? Because it signals that we still want to cooperate and are keen to reach an agreement that works for both sides. We can say 'no' positively, assertively and respectfully.

In a kidnap negotiation, we might indicate a 'no' by saying something like:

'Thanks for reducing your demand. Unfortunately, it is still too much money. Please come down further so we can agree on an amount and get it to you as quickly as possible.'

So, next time you feel obliged to agree to something just to stay in the game, consider some of the benefits of signalling 'no'. You can:

1. **Define your boundaries:** Clearly define personal and professional boundaries to facilitate effective communication by indicating a 'no' when necessary.
2. **Prioritise intentionally:** Evaluate opportunities and prioritise intentionally. Saying no to commitments that don't align with your goals or support your long-term objectives protects your time, energy and focus, and prevents you overcommitting or experiencing burnout.
3. **Communicate value:** Use the power of 'no' to communicate your value. Emphasise that your time, skills and contributions are valuable and deserving of respect.
4. **Strategically use 'no' in negotiations:** In negotiation, strategically use 'no' to set limits, create leverage and contribute to a more favourable outcome.
5. **Practise assertive communication:** Practise assertive communication by expressing needs, opinions and boundaries clearly and confidently.

Warren Buffett, the renowned investor, is master of the positive 'no'. He says no to most investment opportunities and only considers those that align with his investment philosophy. Remember, saying no doesn't mean being inflexible or rejecting all opportunities. It's about intentional decision-making, setting priorities and understanding when saying no is in yours or the negotiation's best interest.

When people feel pressured into saying 'yes' in the heat of the moment, they invariably suffer from the winner's curse or buyer's remorse and later regret that decision. This usually results in cancellations, refunds and rejections – hardly a successful outcome. If you decide to stay, rather than walking away, embracing the power of 'no' can lead to a more balanced, focused and rewarding personal and professional life. This intentional decision-making has contributed to Buffet's success and financial acumen over decades, making him one of the wealthiest (and most content) people in the world.

CASE STUDY #2

Josh had been part of his local community group for over two years. They organised events and fundraisers to support local causes. At first, it felt great – he loved being involved and felt like he was making a difference. But recently, meetings had become tense. Some of the older members, who had been in the group for years, had grown increasingly rigid, insisting their ideas were the only right way to move forward. They weren't open to collaboration, and every suggestion from the younger members, including Josh, was met with dismissal and passive-aggressive comments.

Josh found himself in a tough spot. He believed in what the team stood for and did to help others locally, but the internal politics and egos in the group were beginning to drain his energy. After each meeting, he felt frustrated. He had tried all kinds of strategies to navigate the tension – offering compromises, suggesting ways of working together to solve their problems, and even using active listening to understand the concerns behind their rigidity. Still, nothing seemed to shift the dynamic.

Josh was facing his own version of a 'crisis within the crisis'. While the group's work remained important to him, the interpersonal conflict was overshadowing any good work they were doing. He remembered a piece of advice he had once read: sometimes, despite your best efforts, it's time to walk away if the culture or people aren't willing to change.

After careful consideration, Josh decided it was time to move on. He had looked in the mirror and was satisfied he had passed the 'test'. He'd exhausted all his options to find a way through. Continuing to stay would have led to him feeling only animosity and resentment towards the others. Leaving the group was a difficult choice. But walking away didn't mean he was giving up on community service; it meant preserving his well-being and acting in alignment with his core values. As a result, he soon found another group, with a better operating environment, in which his contributions would be more appreciated.

SUMMARY

In this chapter we looked at how staying calm and making smart decisions helps you get through tough times. While individual skills are important, the ability to work well with others and collaborate is paramount. Human beings are neurologically wired to crave connection and need to feel valued and that they matter to others.

By being kinder and more collaborative when you talk to others, you will build stronger relationships, which in turn will support you when things get difficult. We also looked at

why using harsh tactics like making extreme demands or ulti-
matums might work for a short while, but they rarely lead to
long-term success or meaningful, trust-based relationships.
Being tough just to win the argument can breed resentment,
but working together and seeking mutual benefit makes it
easier to solve problems and keeps people wanting to work
with you.

Understanding the concept of 'hire for attitude, train for
skill', means that having the right attitude, such as being positive, flexible and able to handle stress, is more important than
having the required skill set from the outset. Skills can be taught,
but a good attitude helps people fit into the team more easily.
This is especially important during crises where people need to
trust one other, which can also help when making important
decisions.

This chapter also considered how best to deal with conflict by
listening carefully, demonstrating empathy and communicating
clearly. Understanding and validating others' perspectives,
rather than trying to shift the conversation, also helps build
trust and makes the other person feel understood. This, in turn,
makes cooperation or collaboration more likely.

As we've also established, there's no shame in you walking
away from a deal, job or relationship that is no longer viable.
Often doing so provides you with multiple lessons to learn
about yourself. Equally, if you decide to stay and work through
the issues and challenges, you'll invariably need to have difficult conversations, including those in which you might need to
acknowledge and accept the views of others that you don't like
or agree with. Once you've done so, you've earned the right to
present your own opinions, which might include certain boundaries that are important to you. In other words, you are convey-
ing a 'no' to the other person.

KEY TAKEAWAYS

1. **Work together**: Long-lasting success comes from cooperation or collaboration, not from trying to win every argument
   at another's expense. If you need to walk away, don't take
   too long to do so.
2. **Attitude matters**: A positive, flexible attitude is more valuable than just skills.
3. **Support, rather than shift the conversation**: Listen and
   show empathy instead of just pushing your own agenda.
4. **Build resilience**: Strong teams can bounce back from
   setbacks if they support one other.
5. **Leadership is key**: The best leaders keep their teams
   focused and calm through crises and challenges.

11

Raise the Vision: Know Your Team's Outcome

'We make our decisions. And then our decisions turn around and make us.'

F. W. Boreham

What we'll cover:

- **Stay focused**
- **Preparing for adversity**
- **Trust versus performance**

To succeed in life, you need laser-like focus. No matter what happens, you must keep your eyes on the prize. Remember why you wanted your goal: your purpose, passion and reason for living. This is just as important as actively working towards it. It's also about getting people around you to buy in and match your focus on a shared goal. Make the decision today to focus on what matters: achieving your goal, and crucially, feeling fulfilled in the pursuit of it. With a defined purpose and sincerely held conviction, you can unite multiple people around a common goal. Throughout history, leaders have been the ones who can paint an empowering vision of the future, which others can then relate to and see themselves experiencing or benefit from.

An example of this is US president John F. Kennedy's bold vision to land a man on the moon by the end of the 1960s. This was driven by his determination to demonstrate the supremacy of American technological and political leadership during the height of the Cold War with the Soviet Union. His famous 1961 speech galvanised national effort, uniting government, industry and scientists to achieve the goal.

NASA's purpose during the Apollo programme extended beyond the engineers and astronauts; it encompassed every individual, including support staff. It established a culture where everyone understood their role as being crucial to the success of the overall mission. A famous anecdote reports how when a caretaker was asked about his work at NASA, rather than just saying he swept floors, he reportedly responded, 'I'm helping to put a man on the moon.'

This shared sense of purpose created unity and a collective effort towards a singular, unprecedented goal that had never before been achieved. Each contribution, no matter how small, was seen as integral to the larger mission, reflecting NASA's ability to inspire and mobilise an entire nation.

CASE STUDY #1

The V8 engine roared as my foot pressed the accelerator closer to the floor. Glancing down, the speedometer was touching 120 mph. My knuckles were bone white. I released my grip slightly on the leather steering wheel to allow the blood to flow.

The passenger in the front seat next to me was so relaxed that he might as well have been lying on a sunbed lounger, sipping a margarita. He peered over into the driver's footwell and then stared at me. 'Is it broken?'

'Eh?' I mumbled, too busy concentrating on not crashing as the surrounding countryside hurtled past in a blur.

'The accelerator. If it's not broken, fucking use it,' said the stoney-faced instructor from Scotland Yard's police driving school, reclining back in his seat as if resuming his siesta. Trusting in my training and the 1.6-tonne machine, I squeezed the pedal until it couldn't go any further, and the speedometer nudged 140 mph. Travelling safely, smoothly and at speed was a fundamental skill I needed to master as the new boy on a covert armed surveillance team. We were responsible for locating, tracking and gathering evidence against terrorists who were set on killing innocent people.

'Remember,' the instructor offered. 'No matter how fast or slow you're going, always raise your vision. Keep scanning to the horizon and back. You'll anticipate the obstacles even before they've materialised. If you don't, we'll all die at this speed.' With those wise words, the intense four-week advanced driving course literally flew by. His advice of being able to zoom my focus in and out as the situation determined has stood me in good stead ever since.

I now ask myself whether I need to take a step back and keep a wide awareness on the bigger picture, allowing things to unfold naturally; or whether I need to focus on the detail, fully accepting the reality of the here and now, even if it's not what I want to be happening. From either of these interchangeable perspectives, I can then determine what my next course of action needs to be.

While I hadn't driven cars at such speed in a long time, twenty years later his guidance still played a pivotal role in my thinking and behaviour. Whether I'm negotiating with kidnappers in the jungles of the Niger Delta or delivering a communication skills workshop for a financial service company in Madrid, I'm always raising my vision, zooming in and out as required. This means reflecting on all the potential challenges, questions, issues, etc., that might occur or even jeopardise the session, business deal or key relationship.

STAY FOCUSED

Understanding your team's desired outcome in any situation is crucial because it provides clarity and direction. Knowing what you want to achieve helps you set goals, make informed decisions and maintain motivation, especially when challenges arise. However, equally important is the ability to let go of that outcome and focus on the process. By concentrating on each step – placing one foot in front of the other – you and your team also cultivate resilience and adaptability.

This approach allows you to stay flexible in your response to the inevitable obstacles while remaining open to even better opportunities that might arise. When you're too fixated on the outcome, you might miss valuable insights or become discouraged by setbacks.

Also emphasising the journey over the destination can help reduce anxiety about the future and encourage a growth mindset, where every experience, whether positive or negative, becomes an opportunity for learning and growth. It can also foster a team-oriented growth mindset including building strong relationships.

Consistently high-performing teams are usually good at 'policing' and self-regulating themselves, while also encouraging improvement. They do so by setting clear standards and expectations, as well as fostering a culture of (mutual) accountability. This is underpinned by open communication where everyone is motivated to contribute at their best, while feeling supported to grow, and there is a shared commitment to excellence. This approach also encourages open and constructive feedback and applies irrespective of role or seniority. Taking such action can address persistent issues firmly yet fairly.

Before your team can align on a goal and collaborate effectively to overcome challenges, you first need to clarify your vision and purpose. A brilliant example of raising one's vision for success while working with others is the distribution and screening of the movie of American singer-songwriter Taylor Swift's 2023/4 Eras Tour. Unhappy with the deal offered by the major Hollywood studios, Swift considered her alternative options. Her overarching vision for the tour was to create an immersive, theatrical experience that celebrated the various phases of her musical career.

One option was to bypass the studios and distribute the film directly into cinemas. The tour had sold out and the North American leg had already made $2.2 billion in ticket sales, so she could reasonably expect that the movie would be an immediate hit. Swift paid for the filming and production herself and could market it to her 365 million social media followers.

Swift's parents negotiated the deal directly with AMC Theatres, the largest cinema chain in the world, without lawyers or agents until the very last stages. While Swift stood to make a huge profit from this deal, she deliberately left money on the table because her goal was to make the tour accessible to as many fans as possible. By partnering directly with AMC Theatres to distribute the concert film, she aimed to maintain creative control and deliver this experience to a broader audience without the traditional constraints of Hollywood studios.

By raising her vision, Swift could keep her priorities in sight even if that meant slightly less profit. Working together with her parents and AMC not only provided fans who couldn't attend the live performances with an opportunity to experience the tour but also set a new precedent in the entertainment industry by bypassing traditional distribution channels. Her reputation as a master negotiator is firmly cemented, along with her profile as someone who demonstrates loyalty and value for her many fans.

PREPARING FOR ADVERSITY

Overcoming adversity happens before the tough situations even occurs. Consider the main themes of this book so far. They include training your brain to be resilient by developing a growth mindset, examining your limiting beliefs to uncover what's holding you back, and developing a support system that you can fall back on when times are tough. Lean into the work that you've already done and use your inner strength to handle the situation. This becomes easier the more you prepare yourself. In other words, train hard so you can fight easy.

Why is this so important?

In times of high stress and overwhelm, we rise or fall according to the level of our preparation, whether as an individual or a team. Despite what you might have been led to believe, practice does not make perfect; it makes permanent.

A famous example of this in action involves the American swimmer, Michael Phelps, one of the greatest Olympic athletes ever. His journey to becoming the most decorated Olympian of all time – with twenty-three gold medals – is a testament to his exceptional talent, unwavering dedication and, crucially, his remarkable ability to overcome obstacles. While it may look like

Phelps' success was an individual effort, the role played by his team, and particularly his coach Bob Bowman, was key. Bowman had been coaching Phelps since he was eleven years old and played a pivotal role in developing his technique, mental toughness and race strategies. Their partnership was instrumental in Phelps achieving a historic haul of eight gold medals in the 2008 Beijing Olympics.

However, even the most thorough preparation couldn't account for every eventuality. One of the most iconic moments in his career came during these Olympics when he faced a potentially disastrous setback. During the final of the 200-metre butterfly, Phelps encountered an unexpected challenge: his goggles filled with water shortly after the race began.

Experiencing goggle failure in the middle of an Olympic final would be a nightmare scenario for any athlete. The inability to see clearly underwater could easily derail years of hard work and preparation in a matter of seconds. But Phelps was not just any athlete; he was a master of mental resilience and adaptability.

In the face of this adversity, Phelps remained remarkably calm and composed. Instead of panicking or allowing frustration to consume him, he drew upon the mental strategies that had become ingrained in his approach to competition. Central to his mindset was the belief that he had control over his response to challenges, even those as unforeseen as goggle failure on the world's biggest stage.

Rather than dwelling on the problem, Phelps quickly shifted his focus to solutions. He relied on his extensive experience and muscle memory to navigate the remainder of the race without being able to see anything. Bowman had forced Phelps to train with faulty goggles. With each stroke, he adjusted his technique and breathing to compensate for the lack of visibility, trusting his training and instincts to guide him through the water. Despite the odds stacked against him, he surged ahead with a final burst of speed, overtaking his rivals and touching the wall in first place.

Crucially, Phelps maintained his mental fortitude and determination, refusing to let adversity dictate the outcome of the race. Instead of allowing frustration or doubt to creep in, he remained fully present in the moment, channelling his energy into each successive stroke.

Phelps ability to stay mentally resilient under pressure was not just a product of innate talent but also of deliberate practice and preparation, as well as strong teamwork. Throughout his career, he honed his mental skills through visualisation, meditation and other mindfulness techniques, allowing him to thrive in high-pressure situations.

TRUST VERSUS PERFORMANCE

Trust is crucial in all forms of communication, and it is especially essential when you are working with others to resolve high-stakes and high-pressure situations. This includes establishing trust *within* your team as well as with the other side.

Establishing trust with kidnappers was always critical to securing the release of hostages. Without it, it would have been impossible to reach a successful agreement and release. We achieved this by following through on what we said we'd do, never lying, and demonstrating a genuine concern for the safety and well-being of the hostages. This was at the same time as empathising with the kidnappers, reassuring them that they would get paid (something), if they, too, demonstrated trust by following through with their commitments.

The same applies in all areas of life. You won't be able to influence or persuade somebody until you know what already influences them. This can only be obtained by working effectively as a team. Achieving the right balance between trust and performance, particularly in business, is an art rather than a science. If we can get this balance right, it can lead to a successful outcome of cooperation or collaboration.

The importance of establishing and maintaining trust goes far beyond just kidnap negotiations. There is always a delicate dance between trust and performance in high-performing teams, regardless of the industry or sector they operate in. Their work often requires unwavering trust in each team member's capabilities and an ability to perform under pressure.

In business, establishing trust is crucial for forming long-term partnerships and clients. For the relationship to be successful, both parties need to meet one another's expectations and deliver on promises. Trust is also paramount in diplomatic negotiations. Yet it is not enough by itself. Performance in upholding complex agreements ensures the longevity and effectiveness of international relations and trade deals. Employment contracts require a balance of trust in the workplace. All sides must consistently perform and meet expectations to maintain a healthy working relationship. This balance between trust and performance is evident in securing the release of hostages as well as resolving other forms of crisis or adversity. When it comes to hostages, the stakes here are literally a matter of life or death. It requires complete trust in criminals or terrorists to stick to their word. But as we've established, trust alone isn't always enough to guarantee success. Performance can be measured by how effectively you resolved whatever crisis you were facing – did you do your best to maximise the chances that your version of the 'hostages' came out alive? – ultimately, it's measured by whether they are released and recovered safely.

A breakdown in trust can destroy a business deal or close

relationship, whereas poor performance – for this read poor decision-making or choice of appropriate action – can just as easily erode trust. You can't emphasise one at the expense of the other. They are both evolving throughout your communication, being constantly tested and refined to ensure it all stays on track. Get the balance right, and both sides can walk away happy.

Organisations often prioritise short-term performance goals over long-term trust-building. The lure of quick wins is understandable, and immediate results can be impressive. Yet, they can often sabotage the long-term success of a team if they damage trust in the process. This happens through high-pressure tactics, such as micro-management, intense competition and constant evaluation, inevitably creating an environment of fear and distrust, disengaged employees and burnout.

Performance is your skill and ability to overcome adversity, whereas trust is more about your skills and abilities as a person, famously summarised by the US Navy Seals as, 'Can I trust you with my life?' (performance) *and* 'Can I trust you with my money and my wife?' (trust).

No one wants to work with a low-performance/low-trust person. Obviously, everyone wants a high-performing/high-trust individual on their team. The Navy Seals discovered that the high-performing/low-trust person is a toxic leader and colleague. They would rather hire someone of low to medium performance who they could trust implicitly to have their back, and then train them up over the high-performing/low-trust guy.

Most organisations only focus on measuring a person's performance against some arbitrary metric, yet they have little or no way of measuring somebody's trust level. What this means is that we reward toxic leaders, which in turn infects the entire culture and organisation.

Measuring Trust

Measuring trust within a workplace is more nuanced than tracking objective performance metrics. Ways in which you can do so include:

Anonymous surveys (with scaled responses to statements like)

- *I trust my colleagues to deliver on commitments.*
- *I feel comfortable sharing honest feedback with my team.*
- *I believe my manager supports my development and has my back.*

Peer and managerial feedback

Gather (360-degree) input to assess perceived reliability, honesty and collaboration. Ask how often the individual keeps promises, communicates transparently and supports others. Observation of behaviours

- **Consistency in actions**: Track follow-through on commitments and meeting deadlines.
- **Openness in communication**: Observe whether they communicate transparently and handle conflicts well.
- **Collaboration**: Note how they work in teams, including their willingness to share credit and assist others.

Psychological safety indicators

Measure whether employees feel safe to express ideas, admit mistakes or ask for help, as this reflects trust within the team.

Engagement levels

High trust often correlates with increased engagement and morale.

Turnover and retention rates

Teams with high trust typically experience lower turnover. Compare retention rates and exit interview feedback for insights into trust levels.

By fostering a supportive environment of trust, you'll experience increased employee engagement and creativity, where people feel empowered to take calculated risks without fear of ridicule or subjective criticism. You'll notice people communicate and collaborate more effectively, driving better teamwork.

You'll also keep your best employees for longer. Lower staff turnover saves time, effort and money in unnecessary recruitment and training costs. Finally, such a trusting environment builds an agile workforce that can be flexible, resilient and adaptable to changes and uncertainty.

Influential leaders (i.e. those who are seen as high performers with high levels of trust) do the following:

Set an example: Leaders should lead with integrity, showing trustworthiness and honesty through their behaviour. Actions speak louder than words, and employees look to their leaders for guidance.

Effective communication: Clear and open communication is vital. Leaders should provide clear goals, offer feedback and listen to their employees' concerns and ideas.

Empower employees: Trust-based leadership involves delegating authority and allowing employees to take ownership of their work. This empowerment boosts morale and encourages a sense of responsibility.

Consider these questions and reflect on the answers to increase your trust-based influence.

1. How do you or your organisation measure a person's trust?

2. What can you do to demonstrate your performance ability and encourage others to trust you even more?
3. How can you build more trust while increasing your and others' performance?

Steps to building trust:

Consistency: Show consistent behaviour to build a foundation of trust. Reliability and predictability contribute to a positive perception.

Strategic relationship building: Prioritise building trust by investing time in relationship-building activities. Make them a 'client for life'.

Steps to enhance performance:

Preparation: Thoroughly prepare. This will help you demonstrate your credibility and reliability, which in turn builds more trust.

Setting expectations: Clearly define expectations and commitments before beginning to negotiate. In a kidnapping, this would be the safe and timely release of all hostages, not just some of them. In a business context, it could be that you need to obtain at least a 30 per cent profit margin in the deal. Defining these metrics at the start ensures all sides know the performance criteria and expected standards. It also reduces the likelihood of any misunderstanding later.

Adaptability: Remain flexible and adaptable during negotiations. Effective performance often requires navigating unexpected challenges and changes along the way.

Trust is the bridge. Performance is the path. Together, they lead to success in both personal and professional realms. Regardless of what form of decision-making or dialogue you're engaged in, you must balance trust with performance.

In these situations, trust is more than just blind faith; it becomes the foundation of emotional connection, credibility and reliability between everyone involved.

CASE STUDY #2

In 1980, six armed terrorists stormed the Iranian Embassy in London and took twenty-six hostages, demanding autonomy for Khuzestan province. The siege ended with a bold SAS operation to storm the embassy after the terrorists had executed a hostage. In the assault, five of the six terrorists were killed, and all but one hostage was rescued alive.

Throughout the build-up to the successful rescue, the trust between the police negotiators and the terrorists was fragile yet crucial. The negotiators had to balance the need to build trust with the terrorists – ensuring a two-way, open dialogue would succeed – alongside demonstrating credibility through their performance in front of the full glare of the world's media. Efforts to establish trust also provided the UK police and military time to prepare for a rescue attempt if the terrorists decided to breach that trust, which they eventually did.

In 2004, at the Beslan School in Russia, armed Islamic and Chechen extremists held more than 1,100 people hostage. Negotiators were confronted with the formidable challenge of establishing trust with volatile extremists clamouring for the release of dangerous prisoners. Simultaneously, the negotiators needed to showcase their adeptness in crisis management, delicately treading the fine line between communicating effectively while ensuring the safety of hostages, as well as the ever-present anguish of grieving parents. Despite efforts by the negotiators, the siege ended in a chaotic rescue attempt that left more than 330 dead, including many children.

In the 2023 Israel–Hamas hostage situation, negotiators from Qatar, Egypt and beyond found themselves saddled with the arduous and nuanced task of fostering trust between two sworn enemies, who each wanted the complete eradication of the other. Competing with this was the urgent need to demonstrate a capability to secure the release of Israeli hostages in exchange for Palestinian prisoners, and the flow of humanitarian aid into war-torn Gaza.

In kidnap-for-ransom cases more generally, trust is the foundation for establishing communication channels with the kidnappers. With this foundation in place, both sides feel they can follow through with their part of the agreement. It is the basis for creating a cooperative atmosphere and allows negotiators to gather crucial information and influence the decisions of those in control. It provides a sense of security to both hostages and kidnappers and can provide a path to de-escalate matters if required.

It fosters a belief that negotiators are genuinely working towards a resolution, and that they consider the well-being of everyone involved. However, engagement in these types of negotiations does not necessarily imply approval or agreement with the other side's demands, threats or actions.

Ultimately, these specific cases highlight that while there are no guarantees, chances of success increase when the focus is on how to work effectively as a team (or multiple teams) to bring about collaboration and cooperation.

SUMMARY

In this chapter, we explored the importance of raising your vision and maintaining laser-like focus on your goals, harnessing the power of a team and building trust with others, all while balancing trust with performance. To thrive, it's crucial to keep your eye on the prize – your purpose and passion – while understanding that setbacks are part of the journey.

There is a fine balance to be achieved, with emphasis required on both the process as well as the outcome. Concentrating on taking one step at a time will help you remain flexible and build resilience, allowing room for you to grow while identifying better opportunities along the way. This is far better, and more sustainable, than allowing yourself to be overwhelmed or blinded by your end goal.

Raising your vision and nurturing trust creates a collaborative environment, which is essential for achieving mutually beneficial outcomes. Trust is a foundational element in high-stakes situations where maintaining relationships is vital for success. We've underscored the importance of preparing adequately to handle adversity, and the balance between trust and performance. Taylor Swift demonstrated the power of focusing on the bigger picture by prioritising fan accessibility to her live concerts over just profit. One way she achieved that was by building trust with AMC Theatres (who screened her shows), while also protecting her artistic integrity.

KEY TAKEAWAYS

1. **Stay focused**: Raise your vision. Keep your attention on your goals as well as the present moment. Stay flexible; don't let setbacks distract you from your purpose.

2. **Build trust**: Establish a foundation of trust by being reliable and demonstrating empathy, which fosters collaboration.

3. **Balance trust and performance**: In difficult situations, both trust and performance are crucial. High performance should not come at the expense of trust, and vice versa.

4. **Get your team on board**: It's crucial to get the people around you to buy in and match your focus on a shared goal.

5. **Prepare for adversity**: Developing resilience by preparing well and maintaining a growth mindset equips you to handle challenges effectively when they arise.

6. **Enjoy the journey**: Focusing on the process and learning from every experience enhances adaptability and reduces anxiety about your desired future outcomes.

12

Get After It

'Resilience is the building block of happiness.'
                                        Dr Rick Hansen

What we'll cover:

- **Overcoming barriers**
- **Building team resilience**
- **Team performance under pressure**
- **Thinking effectively as a team**
- **Cultivating collective emotional strength**

In times of pressure and uncertainty, the strength of any team, whether that's in sport, business or even at home, relies on its collective resilience, adaptability and shared purpose. Success comes not from individual efforts alone but from when the group thinks, feels and acts cohesively, almost as one.

Resilience is often seen as an individual trait, but it is equally crucial for teams. A resilient team can navigate challenges more effectively, maintain focus during adversity and recover quickly from setbacks. Developing it involves more than just ensuring individual well-being; it requires fostering trust and ongoing open communication and transparency, where honest, even difficult, conversations and decisions can take place throughout the team.

This chapter focuses on building team-wide resilience that enables all its members to overcome challenges together. At the same time, it fosters an environment where collaboration and mutual support encourage everyone to perform at their best, regardless of the pressures they're under.

OVERCOMING BARRIERS

Disputes in the home, such as those between parents and children, can be particularly challenging. So, how can you deal with these effectively? It begins by approaching it just like you would in any team, with you as the captain. Getting an early night because of school the following day might be a worthy goal for parents of young children. However, kids will often disagree with this (why are teenagers, for example, so difficult to persuade to go to bed in the evening, yet equally challenging to get them up the following morning!) When faced with the inevitable backchat, tantrums and tears, most parents jump between an overzealous laying down of the law and simply giving in out of sheer frustration. We often decide our course of action based on how irritated or exhausted we are in that moment.

The following three steps can help in all kinds of situations, not just when dealing with unhappy children:

1. Take care of *your* emotions first. Your emotions can overwhelm you during stressful times, making it difficult to think rationally and make good decisions. This can lead to knee-jerk reactions that increase conflict. However, this doesn't mean you should hide your emotions when upset. The key is to find a balance between emotion and reason. Just like in professional negotiations, preparation is crucial. Think about the topics that trigger your emotions in advance.

When you feel angry or frustrated, taking the time to breathe and allowing yourself to calm down is sometimes all it takes. Then, try to see things from your child's or the other person's perspective. For example, if your son has inadvertently tracked mud from the front door to the sofa, take the time to pause and reflect for a split second. He may be excited to watch his favourite TV show or be distracted because he had a bad day at school, just like you may be exhausted from work. Consider your child's inner world. This will help you understand their behaviour better. It will also help you gain control over your emotions. Above all, always assume positive intent, even if the behaviour may look anything but.

2. Help the other person manage *their* emotions. As parents, we know children tend to display their emotions more readily than adults. Therefore, one of the best things you can teach them is to self-regulate their emotions. As adults, we find it hard enough to do it ourselves, so imagine what it must be like for a child dealing with all that powerful emotional energy coursing through their body, without any guidance to steer them in the right direction.

If we respond to our children's emotions with disapproval or logical explanations, they may feel ashamed or misunderstood. For instance, if your son starts crying because his older sister gets to stay up later than him, explaining that he'll be able to stay up later in a few years time won't comfort him now. When you help them face minor disappointments, you create a safe space for emotional growth.

3. Listen to learn. Listening deeply is proven to help the other person's mood improve. It also helps you understand and learn about what's *really* going on for them, not just what you might be assuming. Unfortunately, many parents don't listen well to their children. I'm sure their kids would agree. You may be busy, and multitasking might seem like the only option (even though you now know such a thing doesn't exist). Yet, you're not likely to listen properly to your child while you are driving or making dinner. Instead, set aside one-on-one quiet time to find out what's on your child's mind. Listen and acknowledge what is really showing up for them and resist the urge to jump in with solutions and judgements straight away.

Cultural considerations

There are plenty of nuances and contexts to consider when working with colleagues or clients across different countries and cultures, including the inevitable challenges of navigating crises and making the best decisions possible. Innocent and seemingly minor mistakes can easily sabotage potentially valuable deals or relationships. In my experience of negotiating deals all over the world, while we may all be human and have similar needs and wants, there are several strategies that are worth understanding and applying if you want to maximise your chances of success.

It's helpful to remain adaptable, remembering your national culture is only one aspect of your uniqueness. It can still be helpful, however, to understand the world's cultures in three distinct categories, which will help you to adapt how you work with others accordingly.

DIGNITY (USA and Northern Europe): Dignity cultures aim for win-win outcomes as equals, usually with a competitive element. Also, views an apology as a means of assigning blame and rebuilding personal credibility.

FACE (East Asia): Face cultures aim for humility, respect, harmony and self-worth. Views an apology as a general expression of remorse rather than as a means of assigning blame.

HONOUR (Middle East and Latin America): Honour cultures aim to protect family, reputation and self-worth.

Both Face and Honour cultures emphasise building trust and relationships before delving into details. Once you've ascertained which culture you're working with, consider applying the following four rules to get the best possible outcome for your team.

1. **Do your homework**: Read widely and speak to those familiar with the country and culture.
2. **Show respect**: Seek to understand and clarify cultural differences.
3. **Cultural self-awareness**: Be mindful of how others may view your culture, accepting your own cultural influence.
4. **Bridge the culture gap**: Lack of awareness about cultural differences can create a divide; find ways to connect and create understanding.

BUILDING TEAM RESILIENCE

A resilient and high-performing team starts with a shared vision. When every member understands the goals they are working towards and why they matter, their efforts naturally align. A clear and compelling vision can act as a unifying force, motivating the team to push through tough times and maintain focus, even in the face of adversity. This shared purpose gives meaning to their actions and strengthens their resolve to persevere together no matter what.

Equally vital to team success is the creation of psychological safety. A team thrives when its members feel secure enough to express concerns, share ideas and admit mistakes without fear of judgement or repercussion. In other words, does my boss have my back, or am I likely to be thrown under the bus or made a scapegoat? This supportive environment fosters trust and encourages open collaboration, empowering individuals to contribute fully and authentically. Team dynamics also become stronger, and, at the same time, collective problem-solving becomes more effective.

Resilience also requires adaptive thinking, which gives you the ability to reframe challenges and see setbacks as opportunities for growth and learning, having accepted the reality of the situation. This type of thinking also builds flexibility, both mentally and emotionally, and ensures that the team is better prepared to face future difficulties with a greater sense of confidence and resourcefulness.

Another cornerstone of team resilience is reflection. After navigating high-pressure situations, taking the time to evaluate what worked well and what could be improved is essential for growth. By collectively examining successes as well as mistakes, the team builds a culture of continuous improvement, which in turn reinforces their ability to find better ways of doing things.

Finally, collective success under pressure depends on cohesive and disciplined action, where each team member clearly understands their role and how it relates to others. They also need to master their responsibilities and appreciate how their contributions fit into the larger picture. Functioning as a cohesive unit in crises requires preparation, clearly defined roles and a commitment to accountability. There isn't the luxury of being able to coast or hide away amid a high-performing team in such challenging situations. It's why this level of coordination demands consistent effort and inspirational leadership, as it's the key to ensuring the team can perform effectively under pressure and rise stronger from each challenge they encounter.

TEAM PERFORMANCE UNDER PRESSURE

Performing well under pressure requires teams to be grounded, prepared and cohesive in their actions. One effective strategy is to establish shared pre-performance routines that help focus the team before engaging in challenging tasks. Many sports teams gather in a huddle before or during a game, which helps build team spirit and focus. For example, the New Zealand All Blacks rugby team performs the haka, a traditional Māori war dance, to unify the team and intimidate opponents. Teams also practise coordinated drills to prepare mentally and physically. By reinforcing strategies and building confidence in their movements, they increase the chances of carrying out tasks successfully when under extreme pressure.

Within other kinds of organisations, team routines, such as structured and engaging briefings, can also help create a sense of unity and make sure people are focused. By starting from a centred and aligned mindset, the team is then better equipped to deal with and overcome challenges.

Equally important is the clear definition of roles within the team. Each member must understand their specific responsibilities and how their contributions align with the team's overarching goals. This clarity not only minimises confusion during high-pressure situations but also enhances the group's overall efficiency. When roles are well defined, everyone can focus on their tasks with confidence, knowing how their work supports the collective outcome.

We've established that preparation for high-stakes situations is essential. One way of doing this is stress inoculation training. By simulating high-pressure environments, teams can build the skills and confidence needed to act decisively in real-world situations should they occur. This type of training is most effective when approached incrementally, using the 'crawl, walk, run' framework. Starting with foundational knowledge and basic skills, then progressively increasing complexity, ensures that team members develop the competence and experience required to succeed.

Emergency first responders will repeatedly practise Standard Operating Procedures together in training sessions, which helps them all understand each other's role and how to perform better when under pressure, thereby minimising potentially life-threatening errors. Without this gradual approach, teams risk being overwhelmed by challenges they are not fully prepared to handle.

Finally, having robust and agile support systems can play a crucial role in sustaining team performance under pressure. Emotional and practical support among members helps maintain morale and prevents burnout, especially during demanding projects or extended periods of stress. For instance, rotating tasks within the group can keep individuals engaged while sharing the workload. When team members feel supported by one another, they are more likely to stay motivated and focused, enabling the entire group to perform at its best, even under the most challenging conditions.

THINKING EFFECTIVELY AS A TEAM

It's usually advisable to have just one chief decision-maker in a crisis (accountability is important, after all). The burden of responsibility on this individual to make clear and effective decisions can be alleviated by a team environment that encourages open dialogue, where every member is encouraged to contribute to critical discussions. This is because diverse perspectives often lead to innovative and effective solutions, as they can challenge conventional thinking and introduce fresh ideas.

By ensuring that every voice is heard, teams can better approach complex situations with greater creativity. Encouraging healthy debate within the team can also further strengthen your decision-making process. Constructive disagreements, if handled empathetically, help challenge your assumptions and foster a team culture where differing opinions are valued and integrated to achieve the best possible outcomes.

To guide this decision-making, utilising established structured frameworks such as pros-and-cons lists, worst-case-scenario planning, or red teaming (where you play devil's advocate) can help. These tools also provide a systematic approach, to evaluate options, minimise biases and ensure that choices are considered as objectively as possible, rather than relying on knee-jerk, impulsive decisions taken on a whim.

Once a decision is made, it's absolutely essential for the team to remain united on the chosen course of action, especially if it's different to the decision individuals within the team would've taken themselves. Total consensus is not the goal here; effective team engagement and support of the decision-making process is. Everyone can have their say, but then it's up to the chief to make the call, which everyone then needs to get behind. If you're unwilling to do that, then you probably need to leave the team.

CULTIVATING COLLECTIVE EMOTIONAL STRENGTH

Working effectively with others is about more than you just taking actions and decisions; it is also deeply rooted in the emotional cohesion of teams. The ability to support and motivate one another during challenging times is vital for achieving long-term success. Building collective emotional strength begins with celebrating successes together. Recognising and rewarding the team's achievements boosts morale, fosters a sense of shared purpose and reinforces the bonds that hold the group together.

Empathy can play a crucial role in strengthening these bonds. By encouraging team members to demonstrate their understanding of and respect for one another's challenges, it builds deeper connections and creates a supportive environment where team members feel valued. Regular check-ins further contribute to emotional cohesion by providing opportunities for honest conversations about workload, stress and overall well-being. These types of discussions can also help identify potential issues early and avoid them escalating into avoidable crises later.

Leadership also plays a key role in cultivating emotional strength within the team. Leaders and senior members must model emotional regulation by demonstrating calmness and resilience in the face of metaphorical storms raging around them. Remember, emotions are contagious, and people don't want to see their leaders flapping or crippled by uncertainty. By setting an example, they inspire others to remain composed and focused, even when faced with adversity. Together, these practices create a foundation of mutual trust and emotional support, enabling the team to face challenges with strength and unity.

SUMMARY

This chapter delved into the essential qualities that allow teams to thrive under pressure, focusing on collective resilience, adaptability and shared purpose. It emphasised that success is not just a product of individual efforts but of a team's ability to think, feel and act cohesively. Resilience, often viewed as a personal trait, is equally critical for teams, allowing them to navigate challenges effectively, maintain focus amid adversity and recover quickly from setbacks.

We also explored how fostering trust, open communication and psychological safety creates an environment where honest, and sometimes difficult, conversations can take place, enabling teams to perform at their best regardless of external pressures. You should now be confident in being able to work well with others to handle adversity and take other life challenges in your stride.

KEY TAKEAWAYS

1. **Team resilience is essential**: Success relies on collective resilience, trust and adaptability, not just individual efforts.
2. **Foster psychological safety**: Open communication and a supportive environment enables honest conversations and stronger collaboration.
3. **Shared purpose unites**: A clear, shared vision aligns team efforts and motivates perseverance through challenges.
4. **Prepare and reflect**: Use routines, structured decision-making and post-crisis reflection to improve team performance under pressure.
5. **Support and empathy matter**: Emotional cohesion, built on empathy and mutual support, strengthens teams during adversity.

Conclusion

Here we are. You've made it. By now, you should feel equipped to navigate the complexities of life with clarity and confidence. Armed with the right mindset, emotional tools and practical strategies, you should now feel capable of thinking, feeling and acting in ways that help you make better decisions, even in the most challenging circumstances. This is more than just a set of skills; it's an approach to life, one that embraces resilience and personal growth as not just possible but essential. Fulfilment and purpose lie at the heart of this journey, and with these tools you are empowered to take ownership and responsibility for your life, no matter what adversity comes your way.

As you learned in the introduction, at the core of this transformation lie three foundational steps. First, **take the initiative and calculated risks** to actively shape your life rather than reacting passively to events. Second, **foster cooperation and collaboration by working effectively with others**, recognising that we achieve more together than alone. Third, **build trust-based influence** by cultivating relationships founded on respect and integrity. Mastering these principles allows you to transform uncertainty and chaos into clarity and opportunity, enabling you to thrive in both your personal and your professional life.

Your journey begins with **mastering the inner game**. This involves understanding that thoughts are not facts but interpretations of the world around you. These interpretations, and the emotions they generate, are often rooted in the sum of your past experiences. However, you are not a prisoner to your thoughts. By recognising that you are the observer of your thoughts, rather than being defined by them, you gain the freedom to reinterpret your reality.

The **'Three Buckets' framework** offers a practical way to approach this. By categorising challenges into what you can control, what you can influence and what you must let go of, you can focus your energy on what truly matters. This simple mental tool creates space for clarity and peace, helping you navigate even the most overwhelming situations.

From there, you learn the power of **practising positivity**. This isn't about naive or toxic optimism, but a deliberate and intentional reframing of life's difficulties. By focusing on gratitude, seeking lessons within hardship and embracing the concept of post-traumatic growth, you can increase your emotional and psychological resilience. These practices don't just help you survive adversity; they enable you to emerge stronger and more grounded. Positivity becomes a source of strength, not denial, allowing you to approach life with a sense of hope and possibility.

Wise optimism builds on this foundation by balancing hope with a grounded acceptance of reality. This approach encourages radical acceptance – acknowledging situations as they are rather than as you wish they were – while also recognising your tendency to create meaning from your experiences. By cultivating a mindset where you let negative experiences bounce off you like Teflon, while allowing positive ones to stick like Velcro, you can rewrite unhelpful narratives and focus on growth. This balance between realism and hope empowers you to face challenges with a clear mind and an open heart.

Emotional mastery is another critical element of your transformation. Emotional regulation is the first step, equipping you with tools to manage intense feelings and maintain composure in difficult moments. By recognising your triggers, practising mindfulness and observing emotions without absorbing them, you can **build a 'Red Centre' of calm** within yourself, no matter how chaotic the world around you may be. This inner calm becomes your anchor, enabling you to respond to situations thoughtfully rather than reacting impulsively.

Building on this, **emotional tolerance** teaches you how to endure discomfort and navigate the inevitable challenges of life. Chronic stress, emotional vampires and other draining factors can be minimised or managed, allowing you to cultivate a greater capacity for resilience. With time and practice, you develop the ability to weather life's storms without being overwhelmed, strengthening your emotional foundation with each challenge you face.

As you deepen your emotional skills, you also learn to 'stack the emotional odds' in your favour through empathy and alignment with your core values. **Cultivating empathy** as a skill helps you deepen your relationships and create meaningful connections, while acting in alignment with your values brings a sense of integrity and balance to your life. Together, these practices enable you to achieve emotional mastery, fostering a sense of harmony within yourself and with others.

Action trumps everything. Consistent action, even in small steps, is far more valuable than striving for perfection. You've been warned about the pitfalls of the **multitasking myth** and equipped with practical tips for building habits and routines that prioritise progress over procrastination. By focusing on incremental improvement rather than being paralysed by the fear of failure, you create momentum that carries you forward, no matter how daunting the challenge.

Conflict and crises are opportunities for growth. With the tools you've learned, including assertive communication, managing ego-driven clashes and flexing your decision-making muscles under pressure, you can navigate these situations with confidence. See adversity not as a threat but as a chance to learn and grow, transforming even the most difficult circumstances into stepping stones for personal development.

Another powerful tool you can use is the '**mirror never lies test**'. This concept underscores the importance of honest self-reflection, urging you to pause regularly and evaluate your actions and decisions. By slowing down, you gain the clarity needed to make better choices and use life's adversities as opportunities for continuous improvement. This practice not only strengthens your self-awareness but also aligns your actions with your values, ensuring you remain true to yourself even in the face of challenges.

The journey doesn't stop with individual growth. **Success is a team sport**. Collaboration and teamwork are essential for achieving meaningful outcomes, whether in your personal or your professional life. Insights such as **hiring for attitude, seeking cooperation over competition** and **knowing when to step away** from unhealthy relationships or situations highlight the importance of working well with others. These principles extend beyond individual interactions, fostering a culture of mutual respect and shared purpose.

Raising your vision plays a crucial role in this process. Maintaining a laser focus on your long-term goals, both for yourself and your team, provides direction and motivation. Setting a compelling vision not only helps you stay on track but also inspires those around you, creating a sense of shared commitment to achieving something greater than yourself.

Collective resilience and teamwork are the keys to overcoming challenges and achieving extraordinary outcomes. By fostering collaboration, mutual support and shared resilience, you and your team can perform effectively under pressure and emerge stronger from every challenge. This closing message reinforces the idea that resilience is not just an individual pursuit but a collective one, emphasising the importance of connection, support and shared purpose in navigating life's storms.

Remember, you are not your thoughts, feelings or behaviour. Having read this book, are you now convinced that you're bigger and stronger than all your problems? If you believe your problems are too much and you can't see a way through them, life is only going to get harder. But once you are consciously aware of them, no matter how painful, challenging or stressful they may be, nothing that is ever placed in front of you is insurmountable. Your awareness is bigger than any of it; you can deal with it, overcome it and make decisions that will help you grow as a person. Don't believe me? Give it a go and see how things work out. I think you'll be pleasantly surprised.

So, there we are. You've been guided through a transformative journey, learning how to navigate life's complexities with resilience, clarity and purpose. By mastering your inner game, cultivating emotional strength, taking consistent action and embracing the power of collaboration, you are now equipped to face any challenge that comes your way and make the best possible decisions you can. The lessons in this book serve as a blueprint not just for surviving adversity but thriving in its midst, empowering you to create a life of meaning, fulfilment and lasting impact.

KEY TAKEAWAYS

1. **Resilience through adversity**
   Adversity is not an obstacle but an opportunity for you to grow. Embracing challenges sharpens your skills, strengthens

your resilience and deepens your emotional regulation. Facing difficulties head-on is essential for your personal development, allowing you to emerge stronger and more capable.

2. The power of perspective

Your thoughts shape your reality. By reframing negative events and difficult situations, while consistently performing small, positive habits, you can achieve a real transformation. Constructing empowering meanings will enable you to have better emotional regulation and equip you to make clearer, more effective decisions.

3. Personal responsibility

Success in any area of life begins with taking ownership of your thoughts, emotions and actions. While external circumstances may be beyond your control, your response to them is *always* down to you.

4. Connection

Human relationships, whether with colleagues, family or even 'worthy opponents', are fundamental to thriving amid the storms of life. They are also crucial to your emotional and spiritual growth, offering countless opportunities to practise and learn the lessons necessary for self-improvement.

5. Trust, empathy and cooperation

These three qualities are the cornerstones of effective decision-making. Building trust, practising empathy and fostering cooperation are non-negotiable for creating meaningful outcomes in any situation, but particularly during adversity.

6. Purpose and service

A meaningful life arises from aligning your actions with your core values. From this foundation, you can use your unique strengths to serve others, finding fulfilment in the contribution you make to their lives.

Acknowledgements

Having breathed a sigh of relief when my first book, *Order Out of Chaos*, was finished, I was in no rush to write a second, particularly as it had taken me four years. But then the book did better than I, or indeed anyone else, expected. I was inundated with requests to share the insights, lessons, tools and techniques from the book with live audiences, whether through keynote talks, 'fireside' chats or group workshops. And the one question I kept being asked was, 'Can we have more please?'

While I didn't relish the task of writing a second book, the pressure was on to produce something at least as good as the first – a bit like producing the 'difficult second album'. I hope I have succeeded. I needn't have worried, though, as the support and encouragement of the people that mattered never wavered. Specific thanks must go to my agent Ben Clark, my editor Tom Asker and all the team at Piatkus. Also a big thank you to Lisa and Kamara for their multiple read-throughs and suggestions.

Also, a deep heartfelt thanks to all of you who have shared your stories with me, displaying courage in accepting and taking ownership for where you find yourself, irrespective of the circumstances or whose 'fault' it is. The time for blaming, naming and shaming others is over. To have more compassionate, kinder conversations, we *all* need to become better listeners, without judgement. Only by doing so will we ever improve ourselves, our situation and the lives of others.

If you're interested in more resources on the topics covered in this book or would like to continue the conversation, please get in touch at team@scottwalkercoaching.com or find me online. Alternatively, you can sign up for my regular newsletter at: www.winanynegotiation.com

Appendix

Angry	Anxious	Confused	Guilty
Irate	Worried	Mixed up	Blamed
Annoyed	Nervous	Puzzled	Responsible
Cross/Mad	Distressed	Baffled	At fault
Enraged	Apprehensive	Lost	Condemned
Furious	Troubled	Mystified	Regret
Cheated	Dread		Humiliated
Destructive			Remorse
Cheesed off			
Exasperated			
Displeased			

Happy	Jealous	Hope	Disappointed
Pleased	Envious	Optimistic	Let down
Joyful	Resentful	Expectation	Defeated
Delighted	Bitter	Aspiration	Disillusioned
Content	Spiteful	Yearning	Down
Merry			Miserable
Blissful			Crushed
Ecstatic			Tearful
			Blue
			Low
			Deflated

Frustrated	Disgust	Sad	Glad
Hindered	Revulsion	Sorrow	Thrilled
Defeated	Loathing	Dejected	Pleased
Irritated	Contempt	Solemn	Pleasure
Thwarted	Aversion	Deflated	Wonder
		Mournful	Elation
		Sorrow	
		Weepy	

Hurt	Fear	Ashamed	Love
Abandoned	Afraid	Embarrassed	Affection
Betrayed	Alarmed	Foolish	Adoration
Pain	Worried	Trapped	Infatuation
Distraught	Threatened	Inadequate	Devotion
Despair	Weary	Isolated	
Jealous	Alarmed		
	Frightened		

Notes

CHAPTER ONE: THE INNER GAME: HARNESS THE POWER OF YOUR MIND

Harari, Y. N. (2011). *Sapiens: A Brief History of Humankind*. (London: Harvill Secker).

Fox, E. (2012). *The 7-Day Mental Diet: How to Change Your Life in a Week*. www.bnpublishing.com.

Feldman Barrett, L. (2017). *How Emotions are Made: The Secret Life of the Brain*. (London: Macmillan).

CHAPTER TWO: PRACTISE POSITIVITY

Zaki, J. (2024). *Hope for Cynics: The Surprising Science of Human Goodness*. (London: Robinson).

Rosling, H. (2018). *Factfulness: Ten Reasons We're Wrong About the World – and Why Things are Better Than You Think*. (London: Sceptre).

Jamison, C. (2008). *Finding Happiness: Monastic Steps for a Fulfilling Life*. (London: Weidenfeld & Nicolson).

CHAPTER THREE: WISE OPTIMISM

Frankl, V. (2006). *Man's Search for Meaning*, various editions. (Boston: Beacon Press).

Brown, D. (2016). *Happy: Why More or Less Everything is Absolutely Fine.* (London: Bantam).

Camus, A. (2000). *The Myth of Sisyphus*, various editions. (London: Penguin).

CHAPTER FOUR: EMOTIONAL REGULATION

Damsgård, P. (2016). *The ISIS Hostage: One Man's True Story of 13 Months in Captivity.* (London: Atlantic Books).

Willink, J. (2015). *Extreme Ownership: How US Navy SEALs Lead and Win.* (New York: St Martin's Press).

Richo, D. (2022). *Triggers: How We Can Stop Reacting and Start Healing.* (Boulder, Col.: Shambhala Publications).

CHAPTER FIVE: EMOTIONAL TOLERANCE

Huberman, A. 'NSDR, Meditation and Breathwork'. https://www.hubermanlab.com/topics/nsdr-meditation-and-breathwork

CHAPTER SEVEN: ACTION TRUMPS EVERYTHING

Bruch, H. & Ghosal, S. (2002). 'Beware the Busy Manager'. *Harvard Business Review*, February 2002 issue. https://hbr.org/2002/02/beware-the-busy-manager

Huberman, A. 'What are the 8 pillars of mental and physical health?'. https://ai.hubermanlab.com/s/kSJIhvq-

CHAPTER EIGHT: CRISES AND CONFLICTS

Martino, J., Pegg, J., Frates, E.P. (2017). 'The Connection Prescription: Using the Power of Social Interactions and the Deep Desire for Connectedness to Empower Health and Wellness'. *American Journal of Lifestyle Medicine.*; 11(6): pp. 466–475. doi:10.1177/1559827615608788US
US CDC. 'Social Connection'. https://www.cdc.gov/social-connectedness/about/index.html?utm_source=chatgpt.com
Shonk, K. (2024). 'How to Manage Difficult Staff: Gen Z Edition'. 'Daily Blog', Program on Negotiation, Harvard Law School. https://www.pon.harvard.edu/daily/dealing-with-difficult-people-daily/how-to-manage-difficult-staff-gen-z-edition/

CHAPTER TEN: SUCCESS IS A TEAM SPORT

Murphy, K. (2020). *You're Not Listening: What You're Missing and Why It Matters.* (London: Harvill Secker).
Mnookin, R. H., Peppet, S. R. & Tulumello, A. S. (2020). *Beyond Winning: Negotiating to Create Value in Deals and Disputes.* (Cambridge, Mass.: Harvard University Press).

Further Reading

ON NEGOTIATION AND INFLUENCE

Alison, L. & Shortland, N. (2020). Orbit: The Science of Rapport-Based Interviewing for Law Enforcement, Security, and Military. (Oxford: Oxford University Press).

Duke, A. (2018). Thinking in Bets: Making Smarter Decisions When You Don't Have All the Facts. (New York: Portfolio).

Fisher, R. & Shapiro, D. (2005). Beyond Reason: Using Emotions as You Negotiate. (New York: Viking).

Maister, D. H., Green, C. H. & Galford, R. M. (2000). The Trusted Advisor. (New York: Free Press).

Shapiro, D. (2016). Negotiating the Nonnegotiable: How to Resolve Your Most Emotionally Charged Conflicts. (New York: Viking).

Walker, S. (2023). Order Out of Chaos: A Kidnap Negotiator's Guide to Influence and Persuasion. (London: Piatkus (UK and Rest of the World); Cambridge, Mass.: Harvard Business Press (US)).

PERSONAL GROWTH AND RESILIENCE

Bregman, R. (2020). Humankind: A Hopeful History. (London: Bloomsbury).

Calhoun, L. G. & Tedeschi, R. G. (Eds.). (2006). Handbook of Posttraumatic Growth: Research and Practice. (Abingdon-on-Thames: Routledge).

Gawdat, M. (2022). That Little Voice in Your Head: Adjust the Code That Runs Your Brain. (London: Bluebird).

Hanson, R. (2018). Resilient: Find Your Inner Strength. (London: Rider).

Hawkins, D. R. (2012). Letting Go: The Pathway of Surrender. (Carlsbad, CA: Hay House).

Korb, A. (2015). The Upward Spiral: Using Neuroscience to Reverse the Course of Depression One Small Change at a Time. (Oakland: New Harbinger Publications).

Levy, J. (2018). Why We Do the Things We Do: Psychology in a Nutshell. (London: Michael O'Mara Books).

Miller, L. (2020). The Policing Mind: Developing Trauma Resilience for a New Era. (New York: Charles C. Thomas Publisher).

Omand, D. (2022). How to Survive a Crisis: Lessons in Resilience and Avoiding Disaster. (London: Penguin).

Robbins, A. (1992). Awaken the Giant Within: How to Take Immediate Control of Your Mental, Emotional, Physical and Financial Destiny. (New York: Pocket Books).

Rosling, H. (2018). Factfulness: Ten Reasons We're Wrong About the World – and Why Things Are Better Than You Think. (London: Sceptre).

Watkinson, M. & Konkoly, C. (2022). Mastering Uncertainty: How to Thrive in an Unpredictable World. (London: Kogan Page).

Harvard Business Review. (2017). On Mental Toughness (HBR 10 Must Reads). (Cambridge, Mass.: Harvard Business Review Press).

MINDFULNESS AND INNER PEACE

Hulnick, R. & Hulnick, M. (2011). Loyalty to Your Soul: The Heart of Spiritual Psychology. (Carlsbad, CA: Hay House).

Kabat-Zinn, J. (2005). Wherever You Go, There You Are: Mindfulness Meditation in Everyday Life. (London: Hachette Books).

Richo, D. (1991). How to Be an Adult: A Handbook on Psychological and Spiritual Integration. (Mahwah, NJ: Paulist Press).

Singer, M. A. (2007). The Untethered Soul: The Journey Beyond Yourself. (Oakland, CA: New Harbinger Publications).

Thich Nhat Hanh. (1987). Peace of Mind: Becoming Fully Present. (Berkeley, CA: Parallax Press).

COMMUNICATION AND RELATIONSHIPS

Jackson, P. Z. & McKergow, M. (2002). The Solutions Focus: Making Coaching and Change SIMPLE. (London: Nicholas Brealey Publishing).

Kennedy, B. (2022). Good Inside: A Guide to Becoming the Parent You Want to Be. (New York: Harper Wave).

Murphy, K. (2019). You're Not Listening: What You're Missing and Why It Matters. (New York: Celadon Books).

Sandberg, S. & Grant, A. (2017). Option B: Facing Adversity, Building Resilience, and Finding Joy. (London: Penguin Random House).

Sinek, S. (2017). Leaders Eat Last: Why Some Teams Pull Together and Others Don't. (New York: Penguin Business).

OVERCOMING CHALLENGES

Erikson, T. (2021). Surrounded by Setbacks: Turning Obstacles into Success. (New York: St Martin's Essentials).

Erikson, T. (2022). Surrounded by Vampires: How to Slay Energy Drainers in Your Life. (New York: St Martin's Essentials).

Guzmán, M. J. (2022). I Never Thought of It That Way: How to Have Fearlessly Curious Conversations in Dangerously Divided Times. (Dallas: BenBella Books).

Walsh, R. J. (2020). Tune In: How to Create Intuitive Allies in Business and Life. (London: Harriman House).

Watson, J. (2019). Drop the Disorder! Challenging the Culture of Psychiatric Diagnosis. (Monmouth: PCCS Books).

Thrive Under Pressure

If you're ready to build on what you've learned in this book and unlock your true potential, join me for the Thrive Under Pressure Programme™ – an exclusive eight-week virtual course designed for those who want to perform at their peak.

You'll get the distilled, no-fluff version of the strategies that made me one of the world's top kidnap-for-ransom negotiators, now refined for business leaders, entrepreneurs and growth-driven individuals.

In this programme, you'll learn how to:

• Make smarter decisions under pressure
• Negotiate better deals with confidence
• Master tough conversations with ease

Go to www.ThriveUnderPressure.co for early access and exclusive updates.

This is your chance to transform the way you handle pressure.

Index